ANXIETY IN A RELATIONSHIP

2 Books in 1: Eliminate Negative Thinking, Overcome Couple Conflicts, Trust Issues and Jealousy with Emotional Intelligence and Healthy Communication

Emily Richards

© Copyright 2020 by Emily Richards

All right reserved.

The work contained herein has been produced with the intent to provide relevant knowledge and information on the topic on the topic described in the title for entertainment purposes only. While the author has gone to every extent to furnish up to date and true information, no claims can be made as to its accuracy or validity as the author has made no claims to be an expert on this topic. Notwithstanding, the reader is asked to do their own research and consult any subject matter experts they deem necessary to ensure the quality and accuracy of the material presented herein.

This statement is legally binding as deemed by the Committee of Publishers Association and the American Bar Association for the territory of the United States. Other jurisdictions may apply their own legal statutes. Any reproduction, transmission, or copying of this material contained in this work without the express written consent of the copyright holder shall be deemed as a copyright violation as per the current legislation in force on the date of publishing and subsequent time thereafter. All additional works derived from this material may be claimed by the holder of this copyright.

The data, depictions, events, descriptions, and all other information forthwith are considered to be true, fair, and accurate unless the work is expressly described as a work of fiction. Regardless of the nature of this work, the Publisher is exempt from any responsibility of actions taken by the reader in conjunction with this work. The Publisher acknowledges that the reader acts of their own accord and releases the author and Publisher of any responsibility for the observance of tips, advice, counsel, strategies, and techniques that may be offered in this volume.

TABLE OF CONTENTS

ANXIETY IN A RELATIONSHIP

How to Eliminate Negative Thinking and Insecurity in Your Relationship, Overcome Jealousy, Fear of Abandonment, Trust Issues, and Improve Your Communication With Your Partner

INTRODUCTION 3
Chapter 1 *Anxiety In A Relationship* 5
Chapter 2 *Dismissing Negative Thoughts About The Relationship* 13
Chapter 3 *Banishing Insecurities About The Relationship* 21
Chapter 4 *Jealousy In A Relationship* 29
Chapter 5 *Fears Of Abandonment And The Effects On Relationships* 37
Chapter 6 *The Struggles With Trust Issues* 45
Chapter 7 *Forgiving Yourself For Feeling Anxiety* 53
Chapter 8 *Improving Communication With Your Partner* 61
Conclusion 68
Description 69

RELATIONSHIP COMMUNICATION

How to Resolve Any Conflict With Your Partner, Avoid Communication Mistakes, Create Deeper Intimacy, and Gain Healthy Conflict Resolution in Your Relationship

INTRODUCTION 73
Chapter 1 *The Basics: What Is Relationship Communication?* 75
Chapter 2 *How To Resolve Any Conflict With Your Partner* 85
Chapter 3 *Avoid Common Mistakes* 90
Chapter 4 *How To Embrace Empathy* 99
Chapter 5 *Create Deeper Intimacy* 107
Chapter 6 *Gain Healthy Conflict Resolution In Your Relationship And Mend Bridges* 116
Chapter 7 *Tips For Talking About Difficult Topics* 124
Chapter 8 *The Languages Of Love* 132
Conclusion 140
Description 142

ANXIETY IN A RELATIONSHIP

How to Eliminate Negative Thinking and Insecurity in Your Relationship, Overcome Jealousy, Fear of Abandonment, Trust Issues, and Improve Your Communication With Your Partner

Emily Richards

© Copyright 2020 by Emily Richards
All right reserved.
The work contained herein has been produced with the intent to provide relevant knowledge and information on the topic on the topic described in the title for entertainment purposes only. While the author has gone to every extent to furnish up to date and true information, no claims can be made as to its accuracy or validity as the author has made no claims to be an expert on this topic. Notwithstanding, the reader is asked to do their own research and consult any subject matter experts they deem necessary to ensure the quality and accuracy of the material presented herein.

This statement is legally binding as deemed by the Committee of Publishers Association and the American Bar Association for the territory of the United States. Other jurisdictions may apply their own legal statutes. Any reproduction, transmission, or copying of this material contained in this work without the express written consent of the copyright holder shall be deemed as a copyright violation as per the current legislation in force on the date of publishing and subsequent time thereafter. All additional works derived from this material may be claimed by the holder of this copyright.

The data, depictions, events, descriptions, and all other information forthwith are considered to be true, fair, and accurate unless the work is expressly described as a work of fiction. Regardless of the nature of this work, the Publisher is exempt from any responsibility of actions taken by the reader in conjunction with this work. The Publisher acknowledges that the reader acts of their own accord and releases the author and Publisher of any responsibility for the observance of tips, advice, counsel, strategies, and techniques that may be offered in this volume.

INTRODUCTION

Congratulations on purchasing *Anxiety in a Relationship,* and thank you for doing so.

When dealing with anxiety in a relationship, it can be difficult to work up the courage to find solutions that will help ease your anxiety. Please know that anxiety is part of life and will not be completely vanquished despite how badly we may want it to be, but do not let that discourage you from trying. Like courage, strength is not a lack of weakness, but the willingness to confront your weakness and do what you can to stay above it.

Throughout this book, encouragements and reassurances will be provided to help you continue this journey you have chosen to go on. In the beginning, it may feel impossible because you have lived with this anxiety for some time, but it is not impossible. If it was impossible, then you would not be here hoping for answers.

Your bravery and desire to overcome your anxiety in favor of improving your relationship is inspiring. By picking up this book, you have already taken the first step to improving your relationship. As you read along to find the answers you seek, feel free to take breaks, and consider practicing what you will learn. If you feel embarrassed to try it, then see if your partner will be willing to practice it, too. It is less intimidating when you are not alone.

In the following chapters, important matters such as what anxiety in a relationship looks like will be discussed. You will also learn what is considered negative thoughts, how to recognize them, and learn how to dismiss them before they can harm you and your partner. The many insecurities that come with being in a relationship will also be addressed. Also, tips to prevent them from straining your relationship.

In every chapter, advice and relatable experiences will be shared for your benefit. Experiences with handling jealousy in the relationship will be addressed, both your own and your partner's. You will also learn about the fear of abandonment. You will be able to determine whether you or your partner show signs of this fear and how to overcome this obstacle as a team. This subject will strongly tie into the following chapter, which is about trust issues.

As you continue this journey of learning, acceptance, and teamwork, you will learn to forgive yourself and your partner for feeling anxious in and about your relationship. To complete the journey, you will then read about ways to improve communication in the relationship. This means more than learning how to speak up, so you or your partner will know what is bothering either of you. This means learning the importance of listening, understanding, and acknowledging how you and your partner feel about the matter at hand.

I realize there are plenty of books on this subject on the market. Because of this, thanks again for choosing this one. Every effort was made to ensure it is full of as much useful information as possible. Please enjoy!

CHAPTER 1
Anxiety In A Relationship

A young man has found himself in his third committed relationship since his first break-up, and though he loves his current girlfriend, he is unable to shake off the experiences from his previous relationships. He thinks about those times something went wrong in those relationships and often finds himself trying to avoid such mistakes. Sometimes, he swears he hears an ex berate him over something minor, like his dirty socks sitting beside the laundry basket instead of inside.

His current girlfriend seems so patient and wonderful. She has yet to roll her eyes at him when he mixes up the dates or misplaces his keys, yet he cannot help but wonder. Does she roll her eyes or grumble when he is out of sight or earshot? Does she have her doubts about his capability of taking care of himself?

Does she ever regret being with him because he does not seem to have his act together?

Every day, he is plagued by such thoughts. Each day, he feels himself slip more and more until, finally, he finds himself sat down on the couch with his girlfriend. She places a hand on his knee and uses her thumb to rub comforting circles, but all he feels is dread. "This is it," he thinks to himself as his girlfriend sits on the edge of the coffee table before him. "She's going to break up with me because of the wrinkles in my shirt, or because I fell asleep on the couch. Because I did this. Because I did that." On and on, his mind races with all the little things he has done to upset his girlfriend. Still, she sits there, lips drawn, and brows furrowed as she studies him. There is a look in her eyes that seems unreadable to him. It makes his internal panic worsen until he finds it difficult to breathe. He is panicking, spiraling as he hears all the excuses his exes provided for why they would never work out.

"Is something bothering you," she finally asks as her hand reaches up to cup his cheek. She feels his breath hitch just a bit and then moves to sit on the couch so she can draw him into a hug. "You've been acting weird lately. I tried not to ask because I thought you would talk when you were ready, but... Well, I worried. Did I do something wrong?"

There is a lot to unpack for him. He does not know where to start, but his girlfriend understands. She is patient and encourages him to take it slow. They will work through it together. They will make this relationship work because they are happy together. They will overcome his anxieties together.

Like this couple, you will overcome the anxieties in your relationship, too. The first step in combating anxiety while in a relationship is acknowledging. Acknowledgment that there will be almost as many downs as there are ups. It will take time and persistence from both of you to make this relationship work, and the entire time will be tested as you team up against the anxieties that plague your relationship.

The key to successfully maintaining a healthy, comfortable relationship will be working as a team. Understanding that there will be times when it is hard to smile or being patient comfort when one of you starts to spiral into negative habits. Do not let the thought of having anxieties in your relationship trick you into thinking you are unworthy of being in a relationship at all.

The truth is, it is perfectly normal to experience some form of anxiety while in a relationship. It simply means some steps can and may need to be taken to help both you and your partner to feel secure throughout the relationship. According to psychotherapists, relationship anxieties are common, and typically occur at the beginning of a relationship when it seems unclear whether the other party is equally interested in you.

Recognizing Anxiety

What are relationship anxieties? Doctors and other health professionals have determined that relationship anxieties involve intense fears, concerns, or uncertainties about the relationship. These anxieties can be felt in any relationship, not just romantic. Your relationship with family, friends, and coworkers can also be affected by relationship anxieties. In this book, anxieties concerning more romantic relationships will be the main focus.

Unfortunately, health professionals do not have an official guideline for how to treat these anxieties. They have not determined a way to diagnose it either and instead rely on the similarities between relationship anxiety to other forms, such as general anxiety and social anxiety disorders.

But this is not to say experiencing anxieties well after the beginning is uncommon. Events happen that make even the most secure people feel a bit uncertain or concerned about their worth or ability to maintain current relationships. All it takes is one negative thought to put a crack in the relationship. No matter how much trust you two have developed, how well the boundaries were established, or how well your specific communication styles are understood, that one negative thought will be enough to make any person pause and wonder.

It happens to everyone, regardless of whether anyone will admit it. Questions about whether you are worthy, are you disappointing your partner, and if the relationship will last are perfectly common.

There is a married couple out there who have been married for 27 years. They are still dealing with the anxieties the wife harbors. She feels insecure due to her age–she is 8 years older than her husband–and often jealous whenever her husband speaks with a visibly younger lady. Her husband knows about this insecurity she harbors because he has encountered the repercussions enough times to understand and recognize it.

He does not think any less of his wife for it. Instead, he reassures his wife about his love, and the two have remained strong. They talk things through when she calms down, and together, they go through their established routine of working out the emotions, which helps them both to see how much they love each other.

As mentioned before, this is a form of relationship anxiety. No matter how far into a relationship you may be in, it can and will happen. If you allow yourself to suffer relationship anxieties, you may find yourself feeling more emotionally compromised than usual, such as feeling on edge around your partner and possibly saying or acting in ways that you do not mean.

Recognizing Signs of Anxiety and What to Do

Because it is so common to experience anxiety in a relationship, seeing and knowing that you see signs of anxiety can be difficult. Know that such anxiety does not often look the same between people. You must be vigilant as you observe how you are feeling, and what signs your partner may be displaying. Not every example may apply to your relationship, but the point is not to tell you what is wrong with your specific relationship. It is to guide you to understand what you are looking for, and how to see it.

Do I Matter?

The most obvious example of relationship anxiety is questioning whether you matter to your partner. If you have ever asked yourself this, or if your partner has ever inquired if you love them, then you or your partner have experienced a form of relationship anxiety. Questions of worth come often. It may occur in the beginning when you wonder if the other stays with you because they benefit in some way, or it may occur in the middle when you wonder if your partner ever misses you when one of you prove too busy to spend time together.

When questions like these come up, try to understand the underlying cause for them. You or your partner may be feeling insecure in the relationship for a variety of reasons, and the reasons are often found within the question itself. The question about whether your partner misses when either of you proves busy, for example, may mean you are feeling lonely or neglected.

The quickest solution is often a matter of biting the bullet to ask if your partner minds spending time with you for a little bit. You might try discouraging yourself from asking because you do not wish to be a bother, but remember that you are in a romantic relationship with this person.

You would not be in a relationship with this person if you were a bother. Therefore, it is safe to ask for affection to ease your loneliness.

I Do not Want to Be a Bother

Feeling bothersome is also a sign of anxiety. It is a doubt about your partner's feelings for you, which often leads both of you to wonder about the other. For example, if you feel like you would just bother your partner while they are reading or on the computer, then you might decide to give them space. After enough failed attempts to connect with your partner because you do not want to be a bother, you begin to doubt your ability to time any affection correctly until you completely stop spending time with your partner.

This often leads to your partner wondering if something has happened. Perhaps they will worry that they have offended you in some way, or they may even worry that you are falling out of love with them for whatever reason. Could you have found someone else, and that be the reason you no longer choose to spend time with them? Your anxiety may cause anxiety in your partner, which will further sour the relationship.

The cycle of doubt and worry is vicious. When you feel it, you must speak to your partner about it. The only people who can help you through it are you and your partner. If you never hear what your partner is thinking, then how will you know if you are a bother? You cannot and must not assume you are a bother just because you feel like you *might* be one. Do not forget what people say about assuming.

If I Complain, I Will Ruin the Relationship

On the topic of worry, the worry about whether your partner wants to break up is another common anxiety in a relationship. When you are in a relationship, you will feel loved, happy, and never want to lose those feelings of security. Because of this, it is normal to grow anxious about losing that affection after so long of enjoying it.

From this anxiety, you might find yourself unable to speak about any problems or concerns you have with your partner, especially if those concerns are about him or her. You do not want to rock the boat because that would risk the happiness or stability of your relationship. So you stay quiet and do your best to ignore anything that bothers you, such as your partner wearing shoes while lounging in bed or not letting you know when they are going to be late to see you.

If you feel this situation sounds familiar as you think about your relationship, then it is very likely that you or your partner are experiencing this right now. It is crucial to acknowledge this anxiety, so it can be corrected. In a happy and dedicated relationship, the pressure to keep the peace should not exist. You should be able to communicate without fear of losing the security of your relationship.

Yes, it will not be happy at the time, but moments come and go. Happiness, love, and security always return when the air is cleared between you and your loved one. Choosing to allow such bothers to continue will cause you to build up your anxiety until you begin dipping into another form of relationship anxiety: Sabotage.

Signs Sabotaging the Relationship

Sabotaging your relationship comes in many forms. One such form is starting needless arguments or fights with your partner over little things, such as whether dirty socks are in or beside the laundry basket, or whether your partner remembered to take out the trash that day. These are small, harmless mistakes that you may get upset and aggressive over. Another example of sabotaging your relationship is not communicating with your partner when you are upset or bothered. Instead of sitting down and taking the time needed to sort through what issues you may be having over the relationship or whatever other problem that may have come up, you push your partner away and insist that you are fine or that nothing is wrong.

When you push your partner away like this, you are telling them that their opinion or thoughts are not important to you. This is a show to them that, in some fashion, you do not care about them. The reasons you sabotage your relationship are rarely intentional. Rather, this is often the result of you trying to determine how much your partner cares about you and what is happening to you. The results are rarely what is expected, however, and instead lead to broken relationships because your partner does not understand what you want or need from them.

If you have ever felt pushed away like this, found yourself in arguments because your partner was particularly testy, or found your partner pushing the boundaries that you agreed upon. Then you may be dealing with a partner who is unintentionally sabotaging the relationship. It is difficult to realize this when you are the one causing it, so make sure you pull your partner into a serious talk to find out what it is they want or expect of you. Chances are, they are unaware of how their treatment of you is negatively impacting the relationship and hurting you.

Anxieties in General

Bear in mind; these are just a few examples of what anxieties in a relationship look like, so do not be surprised if you begin to see more red flags about your relationship. Again, anxieties happen at all stages of a relationship, so it is not something to fret over. Regardless of what anxiety affects the relationship, there will always be an underlying reason for it. As pointed out with accidentally sabotaging the relationship, the reason is to see whether the partner loves you.

Naturally, not all anxieties are specific to the current relationship. There will be anxieties that stem from past experiences where you have been hurt, betrayed, or manipulated into thinking the previous relationships ended because of you. This causes you to stress over whether you are making the same mistakes as before. Just like how the young man appeared to suffer at the beginning of the chapter.

Once again, if you recognize any of the examples as something you have thought or done, then know that you need to speak with your partner as soon as possible. Your partner may be hurt or concerned about you and unable to say anything about it because you are in a state of mind that does not allow you to acknowledge their needs in the way they need. The same can be said in reverse.

Private Evaluation of Your Relationship

As you think about your relationship, you may find that your partner has displayed–or is currently displaying–signs of anxiety. This book can be used as the evidence or reassurance you needed before daring to bring it up with your partner. Let this book help you show your partner that it is okay to feel anxious, that it is okay to be uncertain, but not to forget the importance of being a team.

When possible, take a chance to sit your partner down and gently inform them about your concerns and suspicions. There is a possibility that your partner is unaware he or she suffers from anxiety, so do not approach the subject by assuming this as fact. Ease your partner into understanding what it means to have relationship anxiety and reassure him or her that you are not upset.

Just as you would want the reassurance and comfort of your partner's security in the relationship, if it were you suffering, your partner will need to be reminded that you are fully prepared to keep this relationship alive and healthy. Once the knowledge of relationship anxieties out in the open, the next step will be working together. Working together to keep the anxieties at bay. This will involve changing thought processes, like stopping yourself or your partner from thinking negatively on a matter by challenging the negativity with facts about the relationship.

It may also involve confronting uglier emotions or issues. Jealousy is a devastating and common issue that crops up in all relationships. But like the married couple mentioned earlier in the chapter, it is an issue that does not have to rule the relationship. You and your partner can work past it, and though it may never disappear like in the married couple's instance, at least you can feel secure that your relationship is stronger than ugly emotions.

It takes a certain degree of trust to open to your partner or have your partner admit to you about having anxiety. It is a major step in any relationship to have this important discussion. Know that this is a conversation that will resurface throughout the relationship because it is important to always remain on top of the anxiety. Once again, health officials have no official guidelines for handling relationship anxiety, so you must be both comfortable discussing the needs, struggles, and worries that will come up because of the anxiety.

The Reality of Anxiety

It may sound repetitive, but the only people who can make this relationship work despite the anxieties are you and your partner.

That said, you both must take the issue of anxiety seriously. This is not a made-up mental illness designed to draw attention to you or your partner. This is as real as OCD, which is a compulsion that no one doubts exist. Compared to how someone who suffers from OCD will impulsively check the locks around the house several times before relaxing, someone suffering from anxiety will be randomly struck by their concerns.

It may strike them in waves and drive them mad because it suddenly feels like they cannot catch a break, or it may be a consistent blow to their emotions as they fret and worry about everything with no signs of the end. The symptoms come without warning and often hit hard. Sometimes you or your partner may feel lucky when the anxiety does not appear for brief periods. Little relief comes from the period when the anxiety chooses not to rear its unwanted head, however, because sometimes the fact that no symptoms have struck you or your partner may cause the anxiety to flare up.

As it currently stands, there are no true cures or fixes to make anxiety disappear completely. It is like having allergies: Some steps and treatments can be taken to make the symptoms less devastating, but there is no means to remove it completely. That comparison made, anxiety can be treated, and there are available ways that can help the involved parties cope with it better.

There is also no rhyme or reason to explain why we feel anxiety, just as there is no logical or rational basis for many of our fears. It is perfectly acceptable, for example, to fear the dark or fear clowns, yet there is a stigma about having anxiety–which is a significant fear or concern about rejection. It is not fair to accept a person's arachnophobia–fear of spiders–but mock that person's relationship anxiety.

A crucial reality you should understand when having a partner who suffers from anxiety: Your partner knows that dealing with an anxious individual can be stressful and frustrating at times. They are aware that their anxiety is lying to them about the relationship and know that their partners will not cheat or leave them, but that does not make it easier for them to overcome the anxiety.

And yes, just as you may wish your partner does not have such anxiety, your partner also fervently wishes not to have it. They do not like having their flight-or-flight instincts triggered over small and not life-threatening instances. They understand better than anyone else that there is no proof suggesting they have something to worry about. They also know better than anyone else how irrational they appear and are acting, but they cannot control it.

That addressed, please understand: It is just as exhausting for them to live with the anxiety as it is for their partners to deal with it. They do not want to go from enjoying a movie together on a shared day off to being abruptly struck by anxious thoughts. The movie and evening are then ruined for them because they are wondering whether their partner is enjoying the movie with them, or if their partner is just humoring them.

It is especially exhausting for them when these symptoms cause physical symptoms, such as insomnia or anxiety attacks. Suddenly, they will feel as if they are making a scene and grow self-conscious of the idea, which throws them further into a panic or worsens their insomnia. It is more exhausting to suffer from anxiety than stand by him or her and try to help them get through it.

There is a therapist, a certain Michelene Wasil, who describes the anxious mind in a way that is easy to understand: "Our minds take over and go directly to the worst-case scenario."

But that does not mean it is impossible for you and your partner to be happy even with anxiety in the mix. There are plenty of successful relationships around the world with people making their relationships work while also dealing with anxiety. They have found the balance to maintain a happy and wonderful relationship while contending with their anxiety. You and your partner can follow their example and make your relationship remain strong and happy, too.

CHAPTER 2
Dismissing Negative Thoughts About The Relationship

A young woman, Erica, has been in her current relationship for a handful of months, and though everything is going well with Jared, her boyfriend, something still feels off. She does not know what is wrong, only that there is something wrong. It is difficult to say when she started to notice it, but she hazards a guess.

Perhaps it started last week when, by unfortunate chance, she and her boyfriend ran into one of her boyfriend's exes while out shopping. The ex was polite enough, albeit loud and not quite welcoming. It was clear that this lady felt no shame because she fearlessly flirted while Erica was right there. One look revealed that Jared did not mind and was not thinking much about it. He was even the first to excuse himself from the conversation and draw Erica away so they could continue.

And yet. Was it just her, did her boyfriend's eyes linger a bit longer than normal on his ex's figure? Could he still have lingering regrets about losing that relationship?

Ever since that day, Erica has compared herself to that ex–at least, to what little she learned that day. Jared's ex was taller, slimmer, and looked like a model with her makeup on. Erica did not wear makeup. She never learned to like makeup, never cared to try it herself, but never judged others for wearing it either. It never crossed her mind that maybe Jared preferred ladies who wore makeup until now.

Should she wear makeup, or would it be too weird? She did not know how to apply any of it, though. What kind of girl did not know how to use makeup? Her self-esteem began to drop as she realized she was not good at girly things, not to mention she did not know how to be girly in the first place. Was Jared okay with this, or was he just humoring their relationship?

He must be humoring it. Otherwise, why would he be with someone who was not nearly as slim as his ex? Where Erica's figure showed that she was not shy about eating but still looked proportionate for her height, Jared's ex looked like a model had graced them with her presence. Why would Jared ever leave someone who looked so perfect?

"Nothing like her," she tells herself as she compares her body to what she believes Jared's ex must look like. "Not tall, not slim; bad at flirting, bad at engaging conversation with strangers." On and on, she compares herself to the ex without allowing herself the chance to think about the positives. With these seeds of doubt sown that day, Erica has found herself overthinking and wondering about their relationship more often. As she continues to compare herself and overthink Jared's commitment to her, the relationship starts to feel strained by both parties. Jared knows something is up, but he struggles to get his reassurances across.

Erica has been second-guessing Jared's actions and words, seeing hints and warnings about his intentions and lack of interest in the most inconsequential and innocent interactions. With Erica so focused on the negatives, both imagined and self-imposed, Jared finds it near impossible to make the relationship. It is supposed to be a team effort, but with Erica mentally occupied by her negativity, Jared is essentially left to defend the relationship alone.

The thoughts Erica is experiencing are unhealthy. They are negative, overpowering, and harmful to the involved parties. It can be difficult to stop thinking negatively once you start, and it is equally difficult to catch yourself in time to help mitigate the problem, but it is not impossible. For Erica, she is unaware that she is overly negative about her situation.

Given this is her second relationship, Erica has never experienced the frustration and insecurities of meeting her partner's ex before, so this is new territory. She is uncertain about what to do and how to handle it, which worsens her negative thinking until it becomes unbearable. The very term, "negative thinking," may even be a foreign concept to her because of her inexperience.

For her, the question may become, "What is negative thinking?" The simple answer is as broad as saying you fear or are unable to cope with the unknown. In a relationship, that typically means fearing or being unable to cope with where you stand in your partner's eyes. Negative thinking causes you to doubt yourself and your partner, leaving both of you confused and on shaky terms.

Emotional Triggers for Negative Thinking

The causes for such thoughts are varied, like a garden and as random as a number generator. Common triggers for negative thoughts include stress, depression, even exhaustion. In a relationship, one of the triggers is what Erica experienced: An unexpected meeting with the partner's ex. Negative thinking can also be caused by something called an emotional trigger, which is the response to hearing, witnessing, or generally experiencing something that causes specific emotions to take over.

An example of this is hearing someone yelling. The yelling could be muffled, but if the person hears it, then he or she will feel an unexpected emotional reaction. If, for example, the person's parents often yelled during his or her childhood, then hearing the muffled yelling could cause the person to react in a fashion like their childhood. Typically, the reaction is fear.

In a relationship, an emotional trigger could be what Erica experienced: Meeting Jared's ex. For someone who often experienced the disappointment of a mother or father letting an ex repeatedly return, seeing your partner's ex show up could be an emotional trigger. This emotional response could be negative thoughts, such as expecting the relationship to end with arguments or violence.

Though there is no reason for this person to fear the relationship is ending just because they met the partner's ex. There is certainly no reason to expect arguments or violence because the relationship has always been peaceful and healthy, that emotional trigger will completely override the logic and facts in favor of the familiar negative thoughts.

Recognizing Negative Thoughts

As mentioned earlier, it is difficult to break free of the negativity once it strikes, but that does not mean it has to be impossible. A crucial step to combating negative thoughts is acknowledging that you are not immune to them. Whether we like it or not, we all have the occasional negative thought. It can sound like, "I hate how I look today," or, "I wish this day would just be over already."

Negative thoughts are unavoidable, within and without a relationship. By accepting that you will have thoughts like these, you already make it easier to recognize and correct your thinking. The first step in change is admitting changes are needed, so by admitting that you have negative thoughts in or about your relationship is admitting that changes are needed. It is a good and healthy step to take. Do not be discouraged that it is a necessary change, however. As the saying goes, "The best things are worth fighting for," and the security you wish to feel in your relationship is worth fighting for.

When starting to confront these negative thoughts, it is important to first recognize what they sound like. Previous examples were general, everyday negative thoughts that are fleeting. Negative thoughts in a relationship usually last until they are confronted and proven false several times.

Shifting the Blame

In a relationship, negative thoughts look more like, "S/He no longer loves me," or start with, "They should…" Thoughts like these are considered toxic, and they should be nipped in the bud as soon as you realize where those thoughts are going. The thought that your partner no longer loves you is presumptuous. You cannot know how your loved one feels if you do not communicate your worries. But that does not mean you should always ask your partner to confirm his or her affections. After enough pestering, your partner may develop their insecurities about the relationship.

Also, finishing the phrase, "They should…" is a guaranteed way to complicate your relationship. You must banish such thinking before it develops into something destructive. Your partner is not a mind reader, so whatever they "should" know, they cannot without you first informing them of it. How will they know you are hurt or dislike something in the relationship if you choose to withhold that information and claim it is fine?

Overthinking in a Relationship

Another form of negative thinking is overthinking the relationship, and the meaning behind your partner's actions or words. When you overthink it, you find yourself jumping to conclusions without proof or reason for such thoughts. These trains of thought often end negatively and have you in poor spirits by the end of your conclusion. Jumping to conclusions because you are trying to interpret meanings out of nothing is unfair to you and your partner.

Unless your goal is to stress yourself out, overthinking every detail is only going to hurt your relationship and mar your ability to trust others in general. It is possible to overthink any detail in the relationship. For example, perhaps your partner returned home half an hour to an hour later than normal from work.

Your mind could easily jump to many unsavory reasons, but unless you ask what happened, you will only make things difficult if you believe your assumptions over the truth. You must not give in to such thoughts. Bear in mind the kind of person your partner is. Remind yourself that your partner has never given you a reason to doubt before. There is a reasonable explanation for every situation; you need only ask to understand.

Negative Thinking is a Habit

After understanding what negative thoughts look and sound like, the next step is to acknowledge that negative thinking is a habit. This habit can be developed as early as childhood. For some, it may have started with always expecting to do poorly on a test. They expected this because they feel unconfident in their understanding of the material. In a relationship, this could lead these people to always expecting their relationship to end unhappily because they are unconfident in their ability in general.

Others develop this habit because of past relationship experience. Perhaps they grew used to their partners always being disappointed in them, so now they always expect to disappoint people and give up on the relationship before ever giving it a chance to flourish. These are all habits–poor habits, but habits nonetheless–that can and should be broken.

Habits are made by choice. If you have a habit of thinking negatively, then you have chosen to think this way. You must be willing to change, break that habit and choose to overcome it. You are better than negative thoughts. The negativity is unhelpful and detrimental, but that does not describe you. You are full of love for your partner and desire security in the relationship. By choosing to dismiss such negative thoughts, you choose to enrich and empower your relationship.

Breaking habits is not easy, so do not be alarmed or frustrated with yourself or your partner if you find negative thoughts creeping back into the relationship. This is not something to be upset about because it will take time to undo what maybe years' worth of a bad habit. Remember to stop, breathe, and praise yourself for catching the negative thoughts in action. You might not have stopped it from forming, but at least you stopped it from becoming a major part of the relationship again.

Fighting Negative Thoughts

When working to break this habit of thinking negatively, the first step is to identify the triggers to your negative thinking. Think about when, where, and why these thoughts start appearing. Do they happen whenever you find yourself cleaning after your partner? Or perhaps you find your thoughts becoming negative while you wind down for the night before bed? Can you think of the source for why these thoughts came to mind? Like Erica, did you see or meet someone who triggered these thoughts?

Once you have answered these questions about your negative thoughts, it will become easier to avoid them; if negative thoughts plague you before bed, for example, perhaps you should consider a different nightly routine. Or, because you know these thoughts are coming, you could face the negative thoughts and counter them with positive or factual thoughts. If the problem is cleaning after your partner, consider speaking with your partner and communicating that frustration so they will become aware of their bad habits.

When you know the reason why your thoughts turn dark, preparing yourself to dismiss them becomes easier. This is a practice known as mindfulness. It means you are aware of your thoughts, feelings, actions, and reactions. This is the practice of looking at yourself, seeing what affects you, and not harshly judging yourself for what you discover. It helps you become aware of your triggers and responses so you may avoid repeating them. If you continue practicing being mindful, you will also learn more about your partner and his or her thoughts or reactions to you. These observations may further improve your mind because you will be reminded of his or her love, loyalty, and other traits that your negative thinking may have previously questioned.

As you practice combating these habits, know that it will take time to break them fully. Repetition is key to forming habits, both good and bad, but it can also be difficult when you must enforce it yourself. Remember that you are not alone because you are in a relationship. Your partner is also there for you, and if you explain what you hope to achieve, then you may be pleasantly surprised to have your partner's support in the endeavor.

Having this support will improve the likelihood of breaking the habit of thinking negatively. If you inform your partner of what triggers you discovered, then he or she can work to avoid them, too. With enough time working together, your partner may also surprise you with observations of their own that will further help prevent negative thinking.

Your Body Speaks Too

If you find yourself unable to avoid triggers because you feel something new triggers you every time, then consider alternative changes in your life. One such change could be your body language. How you hold and present yourself to others greatly affects the way you think about yourself compared to others. When out in public, pay attention to the way you interact, and see if your partner will also observe you.

For example, if you find yourself hunched, tense, or trying to avoid the conversation, then you are more likely to think negatively. Your body language betrays your level of self-esteem, and your self-esteem betrays whether you have a negative mindset. The more closed off you appear by wrapping your arms around yourself or trying to turn away from others, the more you will have bad thoughts.

It will be difficult to change your body language, but the changes will have a dramatic effect on your thought process. You may also need help to improve your posture, so speak with your partner and request help. Reminders to smile, speak your thoughts, or to relax your shoulders will help. You may feel embarrassed or uneasy about the reminders, but know that they come from someone who loves you and is helping because you want to be better. There is no judgment between you two.

Share It, Not Bottle It

Another way to help quell the negative thoughts is by talking them out. Sometimes, our negative thinking stems from strong emotions over subjects that should be discussed. Examples include how uncomfortable you feel when your partner appears so comfortable with his or her ex around, or how frustrated you are about always washing the dishes even after your partner promised to take care of them two days ago.

It often helps to get the emotions out in the open. Talking about it out loud gives shape to the emotion and helps release the pent-up negativity. Once the sources of the negativity are in the open, you and your partner will have a deeper understanding of what is bothering you, why it bothers you, and together, you can make things right. Speaking it out loud brings perspective to the situation that is not available when bottled inside.

There will be times when saying it out loud, adjusting your body language, or anticipating the negative thoughts fail to stop them from occurring. Sometimes, they just rush over you and flood your mind, causing it to race a mile a minute with negative thoughts. When this happens, it can be near impossible to break free of the stream of negativity. You will have to either snap out of it by yourself or your partner or find a way to force calm in your mind.

Some experts claim meditation is a powerful tool that combats racing thoughts. It teaches you how to clear your mind and let go of the negativity that eagerly flows through your thoughts. Even a minute of emptying your mind would help ease the burden of negative thoughts flooding your senses. Once you feel those thoughts slowing down, take that chance to either combat them with facts about reality or replace them with positive thoughts.

See the Whole Picture

Changing your perspective on the matter is also a great way to combat negative thinking. When you start thinking negatively, your mind tends to obsess about that one version of the story. It sees only the part or parts that upset it and systematically ignores everything else. You must remember that there are more sides to the story than what you initially see.

What that negative thinking does is judge a book by its cover, and that habit has never been effective. By changing your perspective, you choose to stop and try to see the situation from someone else's eyes. For example, say your negative thoughts were running wild because your partner came home late from work. The first thought is often an accusation of your partner cheating, but is that even possible?

When you stop to consider your partner's view, you remind yourself that there is a limit to what is possible in such a short timeframe. Your partner was half an hour late, perhaps an hour late at most. Is there enough time to sneak off with a second lover between now and when your partner typically clocks out? Possibly, but is it likely?

To better understand the situation, you would ask your partner if everything is okay. You mention that he or she is never so late and admit that you were worried. Your partner will most likely explain what happened after such an expression. There might have been worse traffic because of an accident, in which case, you can easily verify it by checking the news. Perhaps something happened at work that delayed him or her because it needed to be taken care of immediately. If this happened before, then it may have happened again.

Challenge the Illogical with Logic

Questioning your negative thoughts like this and allowing yourself to see the bigger picture is a powerful example of regaining control of the situation and your thoughts. Questioning why your thoughts believe in one thing and addressing how proof and facts point elsewhere can derail negativity and open positivity.

If there is no discernable trigger for why your thoughts have turned negative, then actively change the way you word your thoughts. If you start by saying, "He should know not to chew so obnoxiously," then you will only grow more annoyed with your partner. Instead, phrasing it as, "Does he know he chews with his mouth open?" By bringing it up as a question instead of an accusation, you may ease your negative thoughts into a more positive state. In this case, it could become a curious thought to act on and see what your partner says.

Seek Help

A final, efficient way to help overcome negative thinking is to seek professional help. There are limits to what you and your partner can do, and it is okay to admit that you have both done all that is possible. Despite the stigma about needing therapy, therapists are trained to help people overcome negative aspects of their lives. There are also therapists for couples who are ready to help strengthen relationships.

If the price of therapy is a concern, then check with your health insurance provider to see if there are plans that can cover it, or if there are therapists who are in-network. You can also check with your employer to see if they offer employee assistance programs. These programs often include therapy, financial advice, and other supports for the family. Another place to check for therapy is your local community center. It has become commonplace for community centers to establish a wide range of health services staff to help residents with any issues.

Above all else, be prepared to slip up. This cannot be stressed enough, but falling back into old, negative habits will happen. This especially happens in the beginning, when the new, positive habits are still fresh and not yet solidified. It is normal and expected to make mistakes here and there. Do not fret and do not develop the habit of guilting or berating yourself for letting it happen.

Treating yourself negatively is as much a choice or habit as thinking negatively in the relationship. It is unnecessary and needs to stop so you can flourish. As suggested before, remember to stop once you feel yourself falling into old habits. Breathe, or steady your breathing, because every breath can ground you back to reality. Forgive yourself because everyone makes mistakes, so it is not something to be ashamed about. Finally, let go. It happened, you addressed it, and now leave it in the past where it belongs.

CHAPTER 3
Banishing Insecurities About The Relationship

Insecurities bother everyone at some point in time. For many of us, the insecurities are amplified when we are in committed relationships, and this often makes staying in the relationship difficult. For one couple, the insecurities both parties are feeling have been getting in the way since day one.

John and Amanda both have insecurities that keep them from growing as a couple. John needs constant reassurance that he is a good partner, that Amanda is happy, and if Amanda is okay. He believes he is getting on his girlfriend's nerves for repeatedly asking about how they are doing as a couple, and though he wants to relax enough to go even a day without having to ask impulsively, he just cannot stop himself. Somedays, he berates himself for bothering his girlfriend and wishes he would stop being a mess and nuisance.

Amanda has doubts about John's commitment for a few reasons. First, she worries about John's constant inquiries. His insecurity about their standing has started affecting her thoughts about where they stand. At the same time, she feels empowered by his questions. It is a strange conflict to feel, but she feels it nonetheless because his consistent worry makes her feel important and valuable. Her greatest insecurity is judging her worth in the relationship.

All her life, she has suffered from second-guessing her value. Amanda has never thought herself good enough, pretty enough, or kind enough to be worthy of a relationship. The day John managed to ask her out was the best day of her life. She feels complete now that she is in a relationship and has a man who is so concerned about whether everything is great between them. It does bother her how often he asks, and though there are times when she hesitates to answer, she still finds pleasure knowing that she is enough for John.

Analyze the Example

Their relationship is full of insecurities and drawbacks that make a healthy, secure relationship seem like a pipe dream. They rely so heavily on each other to validate themselves and the relationship; it is a wonder how their relationship has flourished, or if it ever will. If this sounds familiar– the constant questioning and the empowerment gained from your partner validating everything you demand–then a step back needs to be taken.

These are serious insecurities that have not only taken over the relationship but have taken over lives. In this instance, John's greatest insecurity is being too dependent on his partner. That dependence has led him to rely on Amanda to take control of the relationship and mother him. For John, he might find himself lucky that Amanda is patient and accepting of his need to be reassured so often.

In another relationship where one person is in the position of constantly reassuring their partner, the demands could make the person lose patience. This patience can lead to the person saying something untrue in irritation or escalate into the person calling out the partner for being demanding and needy. When not informed of why the partner is always asking for assurances or why the partner is needy, it makes sense to feel great frustration. Lack of communication makes relationships frustrating.

As for Amanda, her greatest insecurity is her need to be enough. Once again, she may count herself lucky because John feeds that need to be enough every day. But if she tried to mold a different partner into talking up her value, the result would be vastly different. For one, that person would not appreciate having his opinions countered by her whines of disapproval and self-loathing. It would quickly get old for the different partner and, unlike with John, end swiftly with the partner leaving.

How Insecurities Affect the Relationship

When insecurity is not properly worked out or addressed, escalations leading to break-ups run a higher chance of happening. Therefore, it is important to inform your partner about whether you experience anxieties or insecurities once you become serious about the relationship. Everyone who wants to be in a relationship generally wants it to work out in their ideal way, but that ideal is not always shared and is not always achievable because we all have anxieties and insecurities that hold us back. But that is why we compromise.

We speak with our partner and become a team to help keep the relationship strong. There are always ups and downs to contend with, even more, when there are overwhelming anxieties and insecurities to overcome, but it is always worth it in the end. Still, it can be difficult to banish insecurities. No matter how hard we try, they often return with greater force, but that is nothing to be ashamed or guilty of; that is life.

Insecurities affect everyone, albeit differently, and are based on how inadequate we feel and see ourselves. They also feed into disorders such as eating or drug abuse, and mental illnesses like anxiety or depression. They are often irrational assumptions about yourself, too. These irrational assumptions are fueled by negative thoughts and made real when you believe them despite seeing the facts.

In all fairness, though, everyone has experienced some form of insecurity, especially in a relationship. Self-doubt is a common insecurity that is experienced now and then. But this can be amplified into a chronic concern in a relationship. When your insecurities become chronic, your peace and ability to function 'normally' are impacted. This can lead your partner to wonder what happened for you to act strangely.

When your insecurities take control of your every thought and action, the result often leads to your partner either being pushed or choosing to pull away. As your partner pulls away, your insecurities may worsen, and you may find yourself blaming the problem on your partner. You might say that your partner should have tried harder to understand, maybe your partner has always felt the distance, or wonder if your partner loved you in the first place.

The Source of Our Insecurities

These negative thoughts are all insecurities that do not stem from your partner. Though they may worsen after your partner does something you do not like, that still does not mean it is your partner's fault. Insecurities are internal, and all attempts to make them external are attempts to shift the blame elsewhere. It is always easier to blame the world than admit you are wrong.

The truth is this: Insecurities stem from our inexperience with what we are facing; whether it is the first time or the second, we become insecure because we are uncertain about the best way to handle the situation. This uncertainty often leads to a negative state because negativity is the easiest feeling to experience. Your thoughts, therefore, become negative and critical.

We all know the phrase, "inner voice," from kids' movies, shows, and growing up in general, but not everyone knows that we have two inner voices: The inner voice that we grew up learning about, and the critical inner voice. The critical inner voice is the one that comes up with all the negative thoughts and reactions. The critical inner voice is the voice comparing you to the ex, analyzing your body, and evaluating your worth. Because of this voice, it is a genuine challenge to always be happy, optimistic, and confident. Because of this, do not blame yourself for feeling insecure. This voice is also why your insecurity is not something to be ashamed of and certainly not something to blame yourself for exhibiting.

Feeling insecure is not something a person chooses. It is not your fault that you do not understand how to handle the sight of your boyfriend talking with his ex. It is not your girlfriend's fault for not recognizing how uncomfortable you are about your limited dating experience compared to hers. Neither of you can control when you feel insecure, but you can control how you respond to the insecurities and whether you let go of them.

Recognizing Insecurities

To be able to gain control of your insecurities and your responses to them, it is necessary to recognize them for what they are, when they appear. Insecurities are like negative thoughts: They happen without our notice, so it can be difficult to realize that we are allowing it to change how we act in our relationships. To help prevent insecurities from affecting the relationship, first determine where the insecurity stems from.

Low Self-Esteem

An example of what can cause relationship insecurities is low self-esteem or confidence. Of all the insecurities we feel, everyone has experienced a bout of low self-esteem at some point. Some of us deal with it briefly, usually when we are in school, dreading a presentation, while others deal with it chronically.

When you have chronic low self-esteem, you often find yourself shrinking away from making decisions and doubting that you are capable of anything. When you go into a relationship with low self-esteem already established, you will find yourself struggling to find equal grounds with your partner from the start.

Your lack of confidence may leave your partner feeling more responsible and burdened with having to make the relationship work. There are claims that low self-esteem is one of the top reasons why relationships fail, too. This is because low self-esteem often leads to feelings of uncertainty about the relationship itself. When you do not feel confident in the relationship, you cannot expect it to flourish.

Instead, you may find yourself encountering problems that only you see. These problems are often disconnected from the reality of the situation. They are instead based on fears you have developed over the relationship. The low self-esteem or confidence you or your partner experience are typically the cause of these imagined problems. The chances are that you or your partner have invented the problems, so that is why only one of you can see them so clearly.

Caught in the Past

Among the worst insecurities that can take over a relationship is the insecurity that stems from past experiences. A relationship or two that have gone so sour, you doubt your ability to make current and future relationships last longer than previous ones. Such experiences leave you with something called "emotional baggage."

This baggage is the emotional turmoil and negative memories associated with those experiences. This baggage is often heavy enough to ruin a new relationship early on because the baggage you carry is reminders about all the past failures. You will become so focused on what went wrong in your previous relationships that you lose focus on what you are doing right.

You sabotage your new relationship when you drag emotional baggage into it. Not only is this because you are dredging up anxieties and insecurities that are caused by what you have experienced in the past, but because you are not giving your current partner a chance to show that he or she is not like your ex.

Instead, you may find yourself holding your current partner guilty for the actions of your exes. Part of you may be blaming your partner for the pains inflicted by past loves, which is unfair and illogical. By allowing your emotional baggage to control how you act and react in your current relationship, you make it difficult to bond and develop any form of trust with your partner.

Without allowing the opportunity to bond and develop trust, you deny yourself the pleasure of forming a secure and loving relationship. This becomes a self-fulfilling prophecy of failure for you, and it becomes a painful experience that may become emotional baggage for them when the relationship inevitably crumbles under your suspicion.

Bear in mind that you would not be the only person entering a new relationship while carrying baggage. The chances are that your new partner has also experienced the worst in people and is equally wary about how this relationship will work out. It will help to periodically remind yourselves and each other that this is a new opportunity to succeed as a couple. What you experienced was in the past with another person, and this person is your new beginning.

Ways to Overcome Insecurities

Know that there are more insecurities in relationships than the two listed above. But also know that the steps to overcome them do not vary by much. Because insecurities will never completely disappear, it is important to acknowledge that you will find yourself repeating old habits of doubting, worrying, or experiencing low moments. This is part of life and is to be expected. All that can be done is taking a breath, then practicing methods that help ease the burden and pains caused by the insecurities.

The method that helps you settle your insecurities depends on what they are, and how deep your insecurities are rooted. For example, emotional baggage may best be handled by practicing exercises with your partners. Your exes may have ruined your ability to trust future partners, so taking the time to practice trust exercises could solidify the difference between then and now.

If the insecurities stem from deeper, more personal experiences, such as how you were raised, it may be best to see a professional for therapy. Like the suggestion made in the chapter about dismissing negative thoughts, having a professional therapist or counselor to help you work through these issues may be the best step to take. It is unfortunate, but not every insecurity can be managed by self-help. This is because there are certain traumas and anxieties that we may not want to address due to the hardship and pain they cause.

Professionals are taught, trained, and certified to help you ease into engaging with the deeply rooted problems in ways that do not trigger extreme pain or anxiety. They understand how hard it can be to face our troubles and are prepared to walk you through the steps needed to face and let go of past traumas. This can be especially important when you realize you do not want to engage these issues alone.

Respect and Forgiveness

For those insecurities that are not rooted in serious issues, such as traumatic incidents in past relationships or an unpleasant upbringing where you witnessed toxic relationships, learning to respect and forgive yourself can be an excellent first step. Practicing self-respect is a proven method used to reduce the frequency of low self-esteem and confidence insecurities. By establishing a sense of respect for yourself, you emphasize the idea that you are a person who is capable of having up and downs just like anyone else, therefore you deserve the same forgiveness you would offer your friends if they slipped up.

Forgiving yourself can be a difficult step to take, especially when you lack self-esteem or respect for yourself. The ability to forgive requires you to see that a mistake was made, that it was not made intentionally, and to know that you are allowed to let go. You would not want your partner to feel bad because he or she accidentally dropped a glass cup. Instead, you would fret over whether your partner was hurt because broken glass is sharp, and what if something happened to make the glass slip from your partner's hand?

If you can forgive your partner for dropping the glass, you can forgive yourself for doing the same. To forgive yourself as readily as you would forgive your partner, you must take a moment and breathe, so you do not overthink the situation. Too often, we find ourselves psyching ourselves out with thoughts of, "They will be mad if they find out" and, "They will never forgive me for this. I cannot forgive myself."

The problem with such thoughts is the assumption that you are irredeemable. But that assumption is yours and yours alone. If you take even a minute to think about how your partner would react, then you would know forgiveness is a second away from passing their lips. This inability to forgive you is entirely yours, and this is because you do not respect yourself as a person.

To help you gain more respect and confidence in yourself, you must learn to silence the critical inner voice. It is designed to be negative, and you do not need that negativity in your life. If you must, argue with it by lying down the facts. You are a wonderful person with incredible qualities that are appreciated by your partner every day. Your body is not perfect, but there are aspects of it both you and your partner love. You do not know everything, but your partner loves how passionate you are about the topics you do know.

There will always be redeemable qualities that can help you remember how worthy you are of love and respect. As you silence your critical inner voice, you will also practice compassion for yourself. Naming aspects about yourself that you love will steadily boost your self-esteem and will improve your mentality. With enough time, you will begin to understand why your partner loves you.

Remember to be You

When we fall in love and devote ourselves to our relationships, there is one drawback that regularly takes place: We lose contact with other loved ones. There are times when you will become so wrapped up in your relationship that you start to lose your sense of self and develop insecurity from how deeply immersed you became. This insecurity comes from losing your sense of self.

This happens more often than you would expect and is especially common when you are new to romantic relationships. Getting too wrapped up in your relationship often makes setting boundaries and addressing your needs difficult. It can be nearly impossible to discern whether you have a healthy, balanced relationship when you spend your every waking moment together.

By this logic, maintaining your sense of independence can be crucial: Not only are you able to step back and determine whether your relationship is still strong, but it also allows you to maintain your interests and personal goals. To help keep your identity, make time for friends and family, hobbies, and other interests.

Maintaining your independence and identity also ensure that you feel secure in who you are and where you stand in your relationship. Another benefit of maintaining your independence is regaining or improving your self-love, which will also help you work on your self-respect and forgiveness. Learning to love yourself and maintaining that love will ultimately reduce your stress and increase your satisfaction in the relationship.

If you remain completely dependent on your relationship to define yourself, you may develop insecurities about your worth and whether you are becoming too needy or bothersome to your partner. Losing your self-identity can also lead to extreme bouts of jealousy if your partner has maintained his or her identity.

Think about your situation and consider when the last time you visited friends and family when you last pursued a hobby or interest without your partner hovering beside you. Spending time away from each other is healthy and should be encouraged. Consider speaking with your partner about spending time with friends and family, indulging in hobbies, or pursuing interests like taking walks or working out.

Sharing the Burden

Communicating your fears and worries will also help ease the burden of your insecurities. Without fail, there will be times when your partner does or says something that reminds you of something you are insecure about. Unless you inform your partner about the negative connotations, your partner may never realize why you are suddenly self-conscious or unhappy.

The conversations may be uncomfortable to think about and start, but if you put it off, the conversations will only get harder. You will also find yourself feeling more insecure as time goes on because you or your partner will continue to say and do things that bother each other. Though it will be stressful at the moment, finding a way to communicate these problems will strengthen your relationship in the long run.

Admitting and discussing that you or your partner harbors some form of insecurity is a major step in the relationship. It is a major step, like when discussing any anxieties that either of you suffers from. These talks will encourage understanding, acceptance, and trust between you that will strengthen your bonds and improve the security of the relationship.

By sharing the burden of your insecurities, you will also reduce the likelihood of seeing everything as black and white. It can be tempting, for example, to point a finger and pin all the blame on your partner when something goes wrong, but that does not make it right or true. Your partner may also grow defensive if approached aggressively over a problem that may seem obvious to you but is not obvious to them.

Neither of you will be entirely right nor wrong on the matter, so it is important to recognize that there is a grey lining in the situation where the full picture sits. If you are both too busy trying to be right or struggling to get your words out because you are insecure about confrontation, the confrontation will end unproductive and leave you with greater conflict than intended.

CHAPTER 4
Jealousy In A Relationship

Jenny never considered herself the jealous type, not when it came to looks, not when it came to possessions, and certainly not when it came to relationships. When her friends found boyfriends, she was happy for them. When her sister and brother found lovers of their own, she congratulated them and wished them well. Jealous just never crossed her mind, so while she knew it was something people experienced, it was more of an abstract concept in her life.

Up until she met David, relationships were never on her mind. David was one of those kids in class who had the looks, intellect, and popularity that could make a person's head spin. He also always seemed to know what he wanted, and when he asked for it, he also always got it. Even after he started working in the same company as Jenny, he was given the royal treatment and was instantly the favorite of the bosses.

So, when he approached Jenny and said he wanted to date, who was she to say 'no' at the time?

In the beginning, everyone was happy for the new couple, and Jenny was happy too. She was experiencing a relationship for the first time, and while it was weird to spend every day before- and after-work with him, she had no complaints. David was a perfect gentleman who liked to send her a rose now and then in the middle of the workday. He listened to Jenny's concerns about certain projects, helped her prepare for presentations, and often invited her to spend time with his friends and him. She felt so confident in their relationship that, when David suggested they get an apartment together, she readily agreed.

It was a wonderful experience in the beginning. As the relationship continued, however, she started to realize there were a few aspects of her relationship that she never saw in her friends' and siblings' relationships. For example, she was used to spending Saturdays or Sundays with her friends and talking about their relationship, but David did not like that. He insisted Jenny was spending too much time with them and that, if she wanted to continue seeing them so often, then he would go as well.

At first, that did not seem like too much trouble. Her friends had invited their partners at least once so introductions could be made, so surely this was normal. But as time went on, she began losing contact with her precious friends. On the weekends, David was busy elsewhere; he strictly forbade her from going out to see anyone. Strange that he was so adamant about it, but after enough losing arguments on the matter, she eventually let go of her friends. It was not worth continuing to argue.

It was also not worth trying to defy him because somehow, he seemed always to know where Jenny was and who she was with at the time. That level of control and knowledge was creepy and scary, but Jenny chose not to think about it too much. Instead, she focused on the time she had with David now that he was one of the few people she allowed to see.

Granted, it was not as fun to always be at his side anymore. Most of their time together was spent with him obsessing over whether Jenny was thinking about other guys, why she was acting so distant, and insisting she wears certain clothes or makeup to please him. It was not long before Jenny felt overwhelmed by David's presence. The weekends when he was busy, became blessings in the form of solitude. The only condition to keeping this blessing was making sure she never left the apartment.

On those days she is alone, she has also learned how to get in touch with her friends online. After apologies and long hours of catching up, the subject of David finally came up. As she explained David's behavior, her friends grew worried. By the end of the day, it was clear to her that David was a jealous partner. The signs were all there: Controlling her social life, keeping tabs on her location, and monopolizing her team. Even controlling what she wore and when were signs, albeit they were more subtle.

The entire time, she believed David was in love with her, but now she knows that it was not love. It was an obsession.

Bear in mind that jealousy is not a sign of love. It is an insecurity that warps a person's mind in a way that causes the person to view his or her partner as an object or possession. It is a negative emotion that does harbor an ugly form of desire and can be an example of attraction, but it is not an emotion that is found when a person is in love.

Recognizing the Forms of Jealousy

Jealousy takes on many forms, as seen in the example above about Jenny's experience with David. Where the story continues, you would learn how David further poisons the relationship when Jenny voices her interest in separating. The many trials that followed were painful, scary, and eye-opening as Jenny strives to regain her freedoms and escape the growing jealousies within David's insecure heart and mind.

Jealousy is not easily spotted in you or your partner. Until you spend enough time with your partner to pick up on the traits, everything will seem "sweet" and "charming" because your partner will appear to bend over backward to make your day. Bear in mind that jealousy traits are not always as petty as the movies depict them.

It is often more subtle than that. However, that does not mean it is not harmless. Jealousy is an unhealthy trait that can devastate any relationship if not properly handled. It is a trait that can and has led to domestic violence before, too. Do not take jealousy lightly in a relationship. If you have developed some form of anxiety since starting your current relationship, consider whether it is because your partner is a jealous individual.

There may be signs of jealousy in your relationship. While it is normal to feel jealous of another occasionally, it is not healthy to let such jealousy consume you.

To best recognize the many forms of jealousy, you must first understand what it means to be jealous instead of longing or admiring.

When you experience jealousy, you will typically find yourself looking upon the world with distrustful eyes. Your partner will be the main target of your distrust because you will convince yourself that your partner needs constant supervision to ensure they remain loyal to the relationship. Deep down, however, you will know that these beliefs are irrational and unfounded.

It is your insecurity taking control of your mind and, consequently, the relationship. This insecurity convinces you that you cannot trust your partner to be loyal or faithful without your guidance. You trick yourself into believing that, given their freedom, they will stray because they do not know better. Such beliefs leave you, the jealous individual, feeling increasingly rejected and unloved as you strive to control your partner and your relationship more.

Controlling Your Social Life

That need to control often extends to your partner's social life. Seeing your partner at ease with his or her friends may make your jealousy worse for a variety of reasons. You could feel that he or she no longer acts so relaxed around you in comparison, or that your partner seems too comfortable with the people he or she is surrounded by.

These thoughts will lead you to believe that your partner may be interested in dating one of his or her friends instead of you. Though this is irrational because you are the chosen partner, it can be difficult to overcome the fear of being replaced so easily by someone who was 'just a friend.' Because of this, you may choose to take matters into your hands. This can be done in several ways: The first and most common tactic is pressuring your partner to limit his or her circle of friends to one or two people, and these select few must not be someone you suspect is a threat to the relationship. Another tactic that often follows this is encouraging your partner to ignore his or her friends in favor of spending time with you. This comes in the appearance of "reminding" your partner that he or she is spending time with you right now. And that playing on his or her phone is rude.

A third popular tactic is suggesting your partner clean up his or her friends' lists on social media. You might explain that he or she does not talk or hang out with everyone on the list, so it is okay to cut out people who are just taking up space. In the worst-case scenario, you may find yourself going on his or her account to remove people for your partner while he or she is in the shower or sleeping.

If you believe your partner displays any of these traits, then consider further if he or she has attempted anything else that makes spending time with friends feel impossible. One such example would be their displayed behaviors when accompanying you to see friends. The first sign, like what Jenny experienced in the example above, would be your partner's stubborn insistence to accompany you whenever you go out with your friends.

Also, when a jealous partner is still considering or still in the process of cutting people out of your life, he or she may try appearing disinterested or bored about being there with everyone. In this setting, your partner will disregard any attempts to be pulled into the conversation. It will be as if you and your friends do not exist until your partner deems you worthy of existing again.

The more annoyed your partner appears, the more uncomfortable you and your friends will become until finally, someone claims to have prior engagements that they need to keep. Once everyone has split up, your partner will suddenly act like everything is perfect and brings up something he or she is interested in. It will be as if you never spent any time with your friends, and you are just now going out to spend the day with your partner.

Another telltale sign that your partner is a jealous person is how often you catch or notice your partner stalking through your social media. Every time your partner finds someone new who likes or comments on your posts and pictures, you might find yourself explaining who that person is, how you met them, and how long you have known them. At some point, you may even catch wind or sight of your partner, stalking those people for reasons you do not understand. The usual reason for a jealous person to go to that extent is to search for hints. A hint of your disloyalty or desire to date anyone other than your current partner.

Keeping Tabs of Your Locations

The stalking of social media accounts typically extends beyond learning who you socialize with and whether you have an unspoken romantic interest in other people. Your partner may also be interested in learning your whereabouts based on your social media posts and tags. Because everything runs on GPS and is always aware of your location, it is easy for your partner to always know where you are or have been.

This is made even easier if your partner has inserted his or her email and whatnot into your phone. With Gmail, for instance, your partner can use Google's version of Find My Phone and ping the location of any device that has his or her Gmail attached to it. This way, if you are at a WingStop that is a door away from Walmart, but you said you would be at Walmart, your partner will know. You can guarantee your partner will be calling or texting you to demand why you lied and who is with you.

The accusation of cheating will be constant when your partner can locate you whenever he or she pleases. Even if you are where you said you would be, there will always be that inkling of worry about whether you are there for the reason you claimed, or if you are there to see someone. Because of this, there may be times when your partner "happens" to be there too and either runs into you to see if you are with someone or just follows you without you noticing.

If your partner finds him- or herself in a position that does not allow for easy tracking of your location, then you can expect constant phone calls and texts demanding to know that information. It will not matter if you were away for 5 minutes or if you were not early to meet with your partner. A jealous partner's mind will expect the worst in you and demand reassurance that you are not suddenly distracted just because your partner did not accompany you.

Aggressive and Biased Views

The expectation of you being incapable of staying loyal or focused is another sign of jealousy on its own. It is the toxic view that you are hopeless without your partner, and that is why your partner must be by your side every second of the day. Jealous partners have increasingly aggressive and biased views of how everything is and will be in the relationship. If you step out of line at any point, you will know it because of their reaction.

One example is making the "mistake" of mentioning someone that is not family or your partner. The person can be anyone from your past, such as a childhood friend, or someone you just met like a new coworker who is still learning the ropes. If your partner is the jealous type, you may notice your partner becomes tense or defensive. You will know your partner is jealous, based on what they say, too.

Comments that seem sarcastic or give you the clear impression that your partner is not pleased with hearing about someone else–especially if that someone is the same sex as your partner–are clear signs. The comments may seem small at; first, a touch scathing, and at times, perhaps they will feel backhanded. Understand that it will escalate over time because a jealous partner is a controlling partner.

Jealous partners are so controlling; they even grow aggressive when you are preparing to head out for an outing without them. It does not matter if this outing is a family gathering or if you are heading to the bar while your partner is busy. Your partner will find something to argue about or start a petty fight with you until you are either too put-off about going, or you are too angry to stay at the gathering for long. Either outcome is a win for the jealous partner. Either way, the jealous partner has successfully isolated you and prevented you from meeting or socializing with someone else.

As mentioned before, another sign of a jealous partner is one constantly accuses you of cheating. The idea of cheating is a clear and strong possibility in a jealous partner's mind. It is so clear, your partner cannot resist voicing his or her beliefs every chance provided. Even when the accusations are made in a joking manner, know that your partner is serious.

Not only is this a sign of a weak relationship, but it is proof that your partner lacks the trust you deserve.

In some way, the jealous partner will be aware that the relationship is not at its best. You will be blamed for why it is this way, but your jealous partner will not fret about it because he or she can "fix" the problem. A common "fix" is attempting to win you over. Jealous partners tend to go out of their way to demonstrate their appreciation for you, and though it starts as sweet and thoughtful, the meaning behind these demonstrations is selfish:

Your partner wants to guarantee that you appreciate them, too. So long as you are swooning over the gifts and presentations, the jealous partner will feel reassured that no one will ever replace them in your eyes. They are reassured that your loyalty and attention is focused on them.

Monopolizing Your Time

Once assured that you are won over, the jealous partner will do everything in his or her power to ensure your time is taken up by your partner and only your partner. As touched upon earlier, a sign of this is how your partner behaves in public. They do not want to share you with others because that allows too many variables to affect your thoughts about the relationship.

Because of this, you may find yourself constantly explaining what you are up to, how long you will be, and why you must take care of it. If you do not have a reason deemed worthy, then your jealous partner will insist on going with you. This insistence often comes in forms of, "Oh, sounds like fun" or, "Let me get ready, and we can take care of it real quick."

There is little room for argument when a jealous partner gets this way. When a jealous partner tries to monopolize your time, you may notice that you are experiencing certain changes due to their influence. For example, your partner may insist you ignore your friends because you are with your partner right now. This is a controlling behavior that trains you to pay attention to your partner.

Your partner might also subtly train you to always compliment and agree with him or her. Do not be surprised to find yourself being tested in public, too. A jealous partner wanting to gauge your changed behaviors will not be above, causing petty drama in public and expecting you to take his or her side.

As your relationship continues, you may also notice that your partner is checking on you frequently. At times, it will feel like your partner is checking on you 24/7. At the beginning of the relationship, it will appear cute or welcoming to get a few texts throughout the day. A thoughtful, "How is your day going" feels nice, and the occasional, "Thinking of you" is touching.

But a jealous partner takes this further than a few texts that help make your day better. Their texts will almost feel hourly and like clockwork as they gauge what you are up to and what is on your mind. The only way to get peace of mind is by being in the jealous partner's presence.

Addressing Jealousy in the Relationship

It can require a lot of convincing to accept that your partner is jealous but do not use that time to rationalize the actions your partner has taken to secure your affections. Jealousy is unhealthy and has no place in a loving, secure relationship. If you realize that your partner is a jealous person, then you may have to confront your partner about it.

Confronting your partner will require you to take it slow and to be gentle. It is likely that your partner is unaware of his or her toxic trait, so an aggressive accusation can cause your partner's insecurities to flare into a defensive fight. By taking it slow and easing your partner into understanding how his or her actions are unhealthy, you offer the opportunity for your partner to stop and consider how the relationship has developed.

As you ease your partner into the reality of things, maintain a gentle and positive attitude. Approach the subject with encouraging thoughts, like wanting to reconnect and open the lines of honest communication. Talk about wanting to feel trusted and wanting to trust because you want to rekindle the relationship.

You must avoid definitive statements and questions like, "You have a problem" or, "What is your problem?" Accusations will always be met with the jealousy flaring out in ways that further exhibit your partner's need to control you and the situation. If you must mention there being a problem, phrase it in a way that does not make your partner defensive. Try it out in your head and determine whether it would make you defensive; chances are, what makes you defensive will make your partner defensive, too.

Once you have established the problem, attempt to communicate how this has affected you honestly, you must be forthcoming about your feelings, and be patient as your partner works out your meaning. Jealous partners will not immediately understand why you are so hurt by their actions. Providing examples of what your partner has done and elaborating how that made you feel will help your partner better understand what you mean. Encouraging your partner to share their thoughts and feelings on the examples will also help you meet a middle ground on the matter.

As you go through the steps of sharing your thoughts and feelings, take the time to ask for changes. You will have to phrase these questions as requests, not demands. Consider saying, "Will you stop [insert request here]," with a reminder of how it makes you feel. Express that you understand how difficult it will be to change and that you will support your partner.

With communication working, make sure you show that you are listening to your partner's words and watching his or her body language. Make sure you can determine whether your partner is sincere and serious. Your partner's reactions and replies will determine whether there is hope or if you should cut your losses and disassociate with this jealous partner.

If your partner has proven sincere and agreed to try, then acknowledge their agreement by repeating the requests and reaffirming that this is what you have agreed upon. Let your partner know how happy you are about him or her choosing to change and let them know how proud your partner has made you. This is a big step for your jealous partner, so he or she will need your support to make the necessary changes.

CHAPTER 5
Fears Of Abandonment And The Effects On Relationships

Everyone has certain fears deep within their psyche they either do not want to think about, or subconsciously choose to remain ignorant about. These fears, when left unchecked, will control how we view the world, people, and ourselves. These fears are also known to dictate our actions and reactions. An example of this is the fear of abandonment.

Fearing abandonment is a worry that the people you love and hold dear will, for whatever reason, choose to leave you. While it is normal to worry about separating from loved ones, the depth of worry you experience from fearing abandonment can be crippling and damaging in committed and familial relationships. Why and how we develop this fear has been debated by psychologists and other health professionals for years, but several theories are floating around.

One such theory suggests the fear is an unfortunate reaction that can stem from any traumatic event in your life. Like your first break-up when you thought you would have a grand future together, or from your childhood when someone you cherished walked out of your life without ever looking back. It has also been debated whether this fear develops because of some unexpected interruption in normal emotional development. Regardless of whether it is caused by development inconsistencies or problematic social experiences, the fear of abandonment is often permanent.

The difficult part about this fear of abandonment is how it can affect a person at any point in life. This is because the fear of abandonment is type anxiety, and anxieties take root as we develop and experience more of the world. It is most common for a person to develop this fear in the formative years of childhood because this is the time of our lives when emotions hit us hardest. After all, we are so raw and new to life.

Despite this, it is possible and increasingly common to grow anxious about being abandoned as we grow older. For many, this fear grows roots as we delve into romantic relationships. An example of this fear developing during a romantic relationship could be how jealous or critical you become of your partner as the relationship goes on. In certain cases, your fear of abandonment could be severe enough to make holding a relationship impossible. This severity may convince you that it is best not to attempt any relationship because you cannot be abandoned if you are not attached to anyone.

Fear of Abandonment in a Relationship

Another example would be the relationship issue that Ella and Terry are experiencing. Ella's job has her traveling often, so the best she and her boyfriend can do is try keeping a long-distance relationship alive. Terry knew what he was getting into when he entered the relationship. He was the one to confess his feelings, successfully asked Ella out on a date to enjoy a festival together, and voiced reassurances that it would work out despite their different work environments.

Ella, initially hesitant because she knows how difficult long-distance relationships can get, was over-the-moon happy at the beginning of the relationship. From the start, their communication was superb, they spent a healthy amount of time together when they were not working, and they always built each other up when one of them felt down about an incident at work. It was the best relationship she had the joy of experiencing.

Her joy felt short-lived when suddenly, Terry sent her a message confessing how much he loves her, how important and impressive she is, and that he does not want to be a distraction in her work. He goes on to say that, when Ella returns, they can figure out what to do from then on. Ella is stunned as she repeatedly reads the message. From the way this is written, it seemed to imply that he wanted to break up with Ella. What could have happened for him to end a relationship like this? For the rest of the week she has left to spend at her latest job site, she wonders and frets because Terry is not answering her calls or texts.

What happened for Terry to abruptly call off the admittedly secure and stable relationship he had with Ella? It turns out; he developed a fear of abandonment. His fear became so overpowering that it convinced him Ella would call things off and leave him for someone at one of her distant job sites eventually. The only way for him to dodge the heartbreak of such a loss was to be the first to break up.

The logic? The loss cannot hurt him if he is the one to cut the ties. His fear of abandonment is also shown in the message he sent Ella when he gushed about how incredible Ella is and how her work is too important to afford distractions. With those statements, Terry indirectly admitted that he does not feel worthy of dating Ella. Any dreams he may have had about settling down and having a family together were easily crushed by how inadequate he made himself feel by comparing himself to Ella.

Because Terry gave in to his fear and broke up with Ella, the unintended consequence of causing anxiety in Ella took root. Now, she has a degree of abandonment fears because everything was great with Terry before he suddenly cut her off. For Ella, her fear of abandonment will have developed into choosing not to develop romantic relationships with anyone again. For her, she would rather be alone than suffer the pain of having Terry ghost her.

The Effects of Fearing Abandonment in Your Relationship

Maintaining a relationship when suffering from abandonment fears is difficult. It puts a strain on you and your partner if one of you suffers from such fears, and though you may want to feel more secure in the relationship, certain effects from the fears will stop you from entirely committing to the relationship. Because of how personalized the fear of abandonment is, the struggles you face can be the opposite of what others experience. Regardless of what symptoms or signs you experience, the effects on the relationship are generally the same.

For one, the ability to communicate with your partner will be stunted. Your fear of abandonment can prevent you from establishing an emotional connection with your partner. This disconnect will prevent you from having a heart-to-heart with your partner, which further prevents your partner from meeting any needs you may have while also preventing the same of you from your partner.

This inability to feel safe or secured in the relationship also affects how happy you both feel. At the beginning of the relationship, you may believe you have made an emotional connection because you are satisfied with the time you spend together, but as time goes on, you or your partner may notice that nothing has improved. You may notice that the relationship is stunted because your fear may prevent you from moving to the next step.

Once it is realized that the relationship is stunted, your anxiety about being abandoned can worsen and develop other forms of anxiety or insecurity. One such insecurity developing or worsening already low self-esteem. Other anxieties and insecurities you may suffer from include depression, mood swings, and codependency.

Signs and Symptoms of Fearing Abandonment

There are many examples of how badly relationships go when anxieties like this fear take over. The signs are not always clear, as proven with Terry's message, but they can be perceived once you know what the symptoms look like. One such symptom which is easily overlooked is the person's dedication to pleasing others.

At first, it may seem like the person is simply a hard worker and likes to make people happy, but there may be underlying anxiety that drives this person. That anxiety is often the fear of abandonment. This person might be so stressed about ensuring he or she is liked and useful that even the slightest criticism will be devastating.

That sensitivity to criticism is another symptom of fearing abandonment. This is significant because of any form of criticism, like from a simple question about why the person stands so far away during conversations. Or to more complicated questions like why the person is so eager to please. It can be taken as a sign of abandonment. The person will genuinely believe that the criticism is made in disgust and with the intention of separation.

Another sign that shows someone fears abandonment is how long a person is infatuated with someone. As children and teens, it is considered normal to fall in and out of phases or crushes. As adults, the speed in which someone grows attached to another person and loses interest is a sign of abandonment fears. This is not healthy and should be a warning if you have developed an interest in the person. Seeing how quickly this person accepts and lets go of others should inform you of what to expect, so if you want to make the relationship work, you must be ready to work with the person to break that cycle.

This inability to stay committed with others is another symptom of fearing abandonment. When living with abandonment fears or issues, it can be difficult and downright impossible at times to stay in a healthy, committed relationship. This can be because of a variety of reasons, but the person's fear of abandonment is always one of the key issues at the core.

With this person going in and out of bad relationships so often, it may look like he or she has a pattern of unhealthy relationships. This pattern could be difficult to read because such patterns often have multiple uneasy reasons for occurring. When contemplating the person's history with romance, take the signs with a grain of salt because more could be at the core of the problem than the person, and his or her ex would ever admit. In such cases, do not be surprised if the person who fears abandonment automatically blames him- or herself for the failed relationship.

This pattern with unhealthy relationships can also leave the fearful person stuck in a relationship that is genuinely unhealthy for him or her. In a case like this, the person sticks it out because being with someone–no matter how emotionally, mentally, or physically exhausting that person may be–is better than being abandoned and left alone forever.

One final example, but not the last sign or symptom, is how extreme his or her actions may appear when trying to avoid being rejected. The person may lash out with resentment because he or she may feel like the partner does not pay enough attention or provide enough reassurance that the relationship is fine. These dramatic expressions guarantee the fearful person garners some form of response, and it does not matter if the response is favorable. In cases like this, the fearful person acts in a punishing way, which is extremely harmful to the mental and emotional health of both parties.

Fearing Emotional Abandonment in a Relationship

In relationships, signs of whether your emotional state is healthy will become apparent almost immediately. For someone who fears abandonment, the emotional state he or she gives off will be unhealthy and, in some cases, can hint at a fear of being emotionally abandoned instead of physically. This fear of emotional abandonment is another example where your age does not determine whether you develop this anxiety.

For many, this fear stems from emotional abandonment in their childhood. This is often the product of the parents being insensitive toward them in some way, like forgetting that children are neither emotionally or mentally developed and treating them like adults because of it. A child who is held to standards that are unreasonable for children will also feel emotionally abandoned because their ability to express emotions is often stifled when trying to meet those impossible standards.

When this fear develops in adulthood, it can often be attributed to having emotional connections abruptly cut off with a loved one. If you or your loved one have ever lost someone, whether it is an intimate partner cutting ties with you or watching a parent walk out of your life because of divorce, the feelings from that loss may be severe enough to stick with you permanently. The negative reaction from your losses will have consequences on your future relationships. These relationships are not limited to romantic or intimate, either.

The fear of emotional abandonment can extend to your social and professional lives, too, because a type of relationship is required in every aspect of life. When it comes to suffering from fear of emotional abandonment in a relationship, you can confirm whether you or your partner is suffering by watching for a pattern. An example of feeling emotionally abandoned in your relationship could be feeling unloved despite how often your partner says or displays acts of affection.

You may also feel alone despite being wrapped in your partner's arms or disconnected, even as you are engaged in conversation with your partner. Such feelings are symptoms of fearing emotional abandonment, and they occur because part of you is fearful of the connection you and your partner are trying to develop. The fear of emotional abandonment will have you unconsciously pulling away from deepening the bonds you both genuinely want. This happens because part of you fears a repeat of your emotional needs not being met like sometimes that happened before, like when a parent was always emotionally disconnected, or a previous partner always treated you like a nuisance.

Fearing Vulnerability in a Relationship

The fear of emotional abandonment in a relationship can also branch out into other abandonment fears, including general separation and fears of intimacy. A brand of intimacy fear is the inability to allow yourself to be vulnerable around your partner. As explained previously, someone with fears of abandonment will be sensitive and react poorly to any form of criticism.

If your partner is unable to take criticism well because he or she fears abandonment, you may find yourself unable to speak or express yourself honestly in fear of your partner's breakdown. The same can be said in reverse: Your partner, worried that you will leave him or her, may be reluctant to inform you about any insecurities, concerns, or character flaws of his or hers. With both of you trying to tiptoe around your partner's fears, your relationship may never grow into a healthy and secure one.

You need to communicate with your partner about the important details and validate your partner's feelings. To validate your partner's feelings, do not try to immediately offer solutions to help him or her overcome the struggles. You may believe you are helping by being proactive, but that view may be skewed in your partner's eyes.

Your partner is not looking for you to "fix" him or her when trying to be vulnerable with you. Your partner merely wants you to listen, understand, and validate that what your partner feels is real. Otherwise, your eagerness to "fix the problem" will hurt your partner more than help because you will have skipped over the emotion, which will validate the fear of emotional abandonment. Reassurance that you are not annoyed, disinterested, or planning to use this information against your partner will be necessary.

Learning about each other's insecurities, understanding where these anxieties stem from, and accepting the flaws that come with being human is essential in a healthy relationship. If your partner seems unwilling or unable to act vulnerable around you, then you may never truly understand your partner enough to achieve genuine intimacy with him or her.

Without properly communicating, your partner's abandonment fears may further develop into genuine trust issues. This can lead your partner to be excessively concerned and scrutinizing of your actions, reactions, and general disposition. If not addressed, your ability to connect with your partner will slim until it becomes impossible. How to tackle trust issues will be explained in greater detail later in the book.

If you realize that you are suffering from abandonment fears and struggle to be vulnerable around your partner, then take heart that you are not alone. It is not easy to become vulnerable with your partner after years of protecting yourself. It will take time to become vulnerable with your partner, and you will have to ease into it by watching and learning from others.

As you practice vulnerability, remember to check in with yourself to ensure you are not avoiding or suppressing your real emotions. The fear of abandonment may have you subconsciously denying yourself the truth of your feelings at times because you want to protect yourself, so learning to be vulnerable with yourself may be in the future, too.

Ways to Confront Fears of Abandonment

Confronting abandonment fears is a daunting task, especially if you have developed other insecurities like low self-esteem, but it is not an impossible one. To start, you must learn to be kinder to yourself. Harshly judging yourself and focusing on your negative qualities will not soothe your anxieties and fears. It is important to acknowledge that you have positive qualities that prove you are a partner and friend worthy of love and acceptance.

Accepting yourself will allow your partner's feelings to reach you as well, which further assures you that you can and are loved for you. This is a crucial but difficult step, so if you need help, take a chance with your partner by speaking with him or her. Your partner chose to be with you and wants to stay with you, so opening about your abandonment fears is a step in the right direction for forming a healthy relationship.

When you do divulge your fear of abandonment, remember to do so while knowing what you want from sharing this information. Your partner may want to help "fix" you once you inform him or her about the fears, but if that is not something you want, ensure your partner understands that fixing it is not what you are asking of him or her. You also should avoid forming unreasonable expectations for your partner to adhere to, as that is unfair and only feeds your abandonment fears.

There are steps your partner can take to help you stay committed and open up, but requiring your partner to come and go on demand is not a reasonable step to ask your partner to take. That is controlling and emphasizes the hold your fear of abandonment has over you and the relationship. A reasonable request would be asking for help to maintain and build friendships or support networks. This allows your partner to participate on your terms while also boosting your self-esteem and sense of belonging.

The ideal means of managing your fears of abandonment is to seek professional help from a qualified therapist. The counseling provided by professionals will ensure the steps you take, and the results from your actions will be positive for you and the relationship.

Dating Someone with Fears of Abandonment

If you find that your partner has fears of abandonment and was brave enough to inform you about it, then knowing how to help without being pushy will be a boon to the relationship. An easy way to help your partner deal with his or her abandonment fears is starting the conversation when it must be discussed. Your partner will be hesitant and appear reluctant to delve into the details about the fears' roots and effects, so remember to take it slow. Refraining from pressuring your partner to speak with you about it will improve the odds of your partner opening to you about it.

It also helps to acknowledge that your partner's fears are real. It may seem unreasonable or nonsensical to you because you know that you would never abandon your partner, but that is because you know the inner workings of your mind. Your partner is not privy to your thoughts unless you speak them aloud, so it makes sense to your partner to worry. The best way to assuage your partner is with patient reassurances that you have no intention of abandonment.

Demonstrations of your loyalty can be anything–from gentle reminders that you are there even when your partner feels disconnected to helping your partner be mindful and kind to him- or herself. When you are uncertain about whether your efforts are helping or are simply lost about how to start, remember to ask your partner what they want. It may be an unexpected question that causes your partner to pause and think. Understand that this is good because it means your partner is now practicing self-kindness by acknowledging personal wants or needs without belittling thoughts.

Finally, as a partner, you have the power to suggest therapy. The idea of needing professional help can be daunting or embarrassing, so expect your partner to react unfavorably about the idea. If you can see that everything you both have worked at is not enough, then gentle pushes toward therapy may be necessary. But you must be gentle and let your partner make the final decision. It may help if you go to therapy with your partner or if you have experience going to therapy yourself. Consider offers to look for qualified therapists together and float the idea of just browsing without pressure to see anyone.

CHAPTER 6
The Struggles With Trust Issues

The ability to trust your partner is crucial in maintaining a successful, secure relationship, but contrary to some beliefs, trust must still be earned between you and your partner. Just because you have agreed to start dating and test the waters does not mean you should blindly trust your partner with your deepest, darkest secrets. A healthy level of doubt is expected in a relationship when you are still getting to know each other. That does not mean you should harbor doubts about every little thing your partner does or says. With enough time spent together, you should feel comfortable enough to be vulnerable together. After all, based on all relationships, trust is what keeps a secure relationship stable and strong. Without it, there is no feeling of safety or comfort to be gained in each other's presence.

Feeling uncertain about whether your partner can be trusted despite having no rational reason to doubt him or her is a sign of having trust issues. These issues often stem from past experiences of lovers betraying your trust in some fashion, or having your trust betrayed by a close family or friend. The cause of your trust issues can be from any point in your life. Traumatic experiences are not limited to childhood or adulthood.

When your trust is betrayed once, it becomes difficult to trust others with the secrets or parts of you that the betrayer knew. This excuses your initial hesitancy about sharing such information with your current partner, but if you continue to doubt and convince yourself that the irrational thoughts hold, then you are allowing trust issues to stain your relationship. Allowing your trust issues to cloud your judgment opens doors for other issues to settle into your relationship. If left unresolved or unchecked, then your relationship may become an example of self-prophecy where the relationship ended how you expected it to, but only because your actions forced it in that direction.

Trust issues show themselves in a variety of ways, many of which are internal. For example, if a previous lover betrayed you because he or she cheated on you, you may worry about your partner being away for too long. On mornings or evenings, when your partner returns late from work, your mind may automatically assume he or she was sneaking around with a second lover. It will not matter that your partner has always been loyal, and you have never been given reason to suspect it. Your trust issues force you to remember your last lover's betrayal and colors your current relationship with that betrayal.

For another person, the trust issues may stem from having watched someone walk out of his or her life. A middle schooler, for example, used to live happily with his parents until he turned 12. Around that time, his parents began to argue, which escalated to yelling, which further escalated to threats and whatnot. He used to stay up late at night to listen to his parents' fight until, one day, he woke up to doors slamming.

By the time he made it to the living room, his mother was at the opened front door, a bag packed, and seething. She barely glanced in her son's direction before turning and leaving forever. The boy is nearly done with middle school now, but his mother is still absent in his life. In her place, women have come and gone often enough for him to lose count.

Now, he trusts no woman will ever stay in his father's arms and believes there will never be a mother figure in his life. He has grown accustomed to women walking out of their house, and when he starts dating, he does so with the firm belief that no woman will stick around. His trust issues towards women are too deeply ingrained for him to expect anything else.

Developing Trust Issues

In both examples, the trust issues stem from a previous experience where the trust was betrayed. For both individuals, the experiences were traumatizing enough to permanently color their view on relationships, which in turn made maintaining stable and secure relationships difficult. As proven by the examples above, you can be any age, and your trust issues can be developed because of any reason.

It is more common to develop trust issues from a young age. This is because you are still in the developing stages of your life, so any events that trigger strong emotions or consequences will leave a longer-lasting impression. That does not mean trust issues stem only from traumatic experiences, though. The lack of acceptance, attention, and care can also be enough for a child to develop trust issues that last well into adulthood. For children, trust issues often take root due to experiences in school. Being bullied, ridiculed, or rejected by peers is traumatizing in its way and can be enough for mistreated individuals to carry heavy doubt about why others would want to date them, not to mention be seen with them. This worsens when adults also fail to address the mistreatments by choosing to turn a blind eye or just being ignorant despite seeing the signs, like no one wanting to partner with the mistreated individuals during group projects.

At any point in life, you may find yourself suffering from trust issues because you have developed or lived with low self-esteem. Self-esteem is an aspect of your character that will affect every part of your life, so maintaining healthy self-esteem is crucial in having a successful and happy relationship. This is not limited to romantic relationships; your relationship with friends, family, and yourself are also affected by your self-esteem.

When you do not value yourself because all you see are the flaws and insecurities, you will find it unbelievable that others would want to date or marry you. Losing sight of your value makes it harder to trust anyone to see your value as well. This makes you more susceptible to believing in the worst of others, thus tricking yourself into believing that your partner's tardiness means he or she is cheating, that your partner is disinterested in the relationship because he or she is busy with an activity, et cetera.

A final example of how trust issues are developed, but not to be assumed as the end of all possibilities, is suffering from Posttraumatic Stress (PTSD). There will be times in your life where the trauma is so severe that you simply cannot bring yourself to trust others. It is too painful, too risky, and you would rather protect yourself through isolation than ever become dependent on someone who will ultimately betray you like what happened in your traumatic experience.

Anxieties, Insecurities, and More Associated with Trust Issues

As you can see, trust issues can often be found closely connected with other anxieties and insecurities. PTSD and low self-esteem are two powerful examples to consider but know that trust issues are associated with so much more. For example, depression appears to be deeply integrated with many of the anxieties and insecurities involved in relationships. Depression can and is a devastating disability to live with, and it has only worsened over the years in the United States. This condition makes it difficult to be happy and alters your thought process in ways that make trust issues more likely because, when feeling sad or empty, the negatives in life become easiest to associate with.

Another anxiety that is often tied to trust issues is the fear of abandonment, as explained in the previous chapter. This also means you run the risk of suffering from attachment issues. Such problems can cause you to have difficulty forming a meaningful or genuine connection in your life. They can also cause you to feel crippling anxiety whenever your partner is away because you feel lost and upset when alone.

The fear of abandonment, attachment issues, and trust issues all share a connection with another issue: The inability to adjust to changes or life transitions. Changes happen every day for everyone, but this can be stressful and difficult to accept for people with the mentioned anxieties and insecurities above.

When you struggle with adjusting to changes and life transitions, it means even the positive changes in your life can be stressful and potentially cause panic attacks. Suffering such stress when small and major changes occur in your life will make adjusting to being in a relationship extremely difficult. You may not feel comfortable confiding in your partner because you are not used to having someone to depend on, which plays into your inability to trust others.

You might also find yourself dealing with increased levels of general anxiety when you suffer from trust issues. This is to be expected in cases where you believe your partner is cheating or is lying to you despite having no rational reason to believe it. As your distrust grows in the relationship, you can expect it to spill into your relationship with others. Friends, coworkers, and family members may suffer as your trust issues begin to change the way you perceive everyone. Which will lead you to mistrust everyone and potentially believing they are all aware of what your partner is doing behind your back.

The worse your trust issues become, the less affectionate you may find yourself toward your partner. Your strong belief and mistrust of your partner's words and actions can make it difficult to want intimacy because you will be focused on the betrayal of your trust and how wronged you feel. As you become less physically affectionate with your partner, your trust issues can worsen because you may find blame in your partner for the declining intimacy in the relationship.

Signs Your Partner Has Trust Issues

Trust issues are not fun for either party, but it can be particularly devastating when you are on the receiving end of the struggle. If you suspect your partner is suffering from trust issues, consider whether he or she has directed the following signs at you:

Some days, it feels like your partner is waiting for you to make a mistake, so he or she can get upset. You might feel like you are walking on eggshells in the relationship because you never know what will trigger the unfounded accusations of cheating, being unhappy, and other hurtful comments. It almost feels like you can do nothing right to make your partner happy because he or she will always see something that has gone wrong instead of anything you have tried to do right.

There may also be days when it feels like your partner is giving mixed signals about what he or she wants from you. For example, one moment, your partner may want you close, but then your partner will look at you strangely and abruptly put distance between you. You do not know what happened to cause your partner drawback, but you do know that you did nothing despite being judged so harshly for something you do not understand.

An extreme sign of your partner struggling with trust issues is if your partner seems to lie often, or can be unnervingly loose about the truth. For example, your partner may tell small fibs or absolute lies when you ask or attempt to address certain issues in general or in the relationship. The fact that your partner feels the need to lie about anything is a sign of struggling to trust.

You should not take this personally. Instead, it is best to understand that your partner is trying to protect him- or herself. This desperation to not allow anything hurt him- or herself often skews your partner's understanding and view of what is true into something cynical. This jaded view and need to lie are not done intentionally to hurt you or sabotage the relationship. This is technically your partner's subconscious attempt not to repeat past mistakes.

Another example of your partner harboring trust issues is his or her resistance to moving the relationship to the next step. This sign can be more subtle than the rest because it is generally expected to take the relationship slow to ensure you are both comfortable with moving forward. To notice this sign, you should think about whether your relationship has moved forward at all. Or if the relationship has been stagnant for some time.

If, for example, you have found yourself wondering whether your partner seriously wants to be in a relationship, then your partner's trust issues may be halting your progress as a couple. Your partner's inability to take any steps forward with the relationship–be it moving in together, becoming intimate, or discussing expectations within the relationship–is a direct sign of trust issues because your partner is revealing his or her unease about committing. This is not usually because he or she does not want to be in the relationship, so when you find yourself questioning your partner's interest, know that your partner is having a mental block about the future and not trying to get out of the relationship.

Symptoms of Having Trust Issues

Seeing the signs of your partner suffering from trust issues is often easier than seeing them in yourself. To see it within yourself, you must take a moment and seriously reflect on your thought patterns and address whether there is a real foundation to the patterns, or if the foundation is an illusion you crafted. The first step to determining whether you suffer from trust issues by first addressing whether you believe what others tell you.

For example, if your partner says he or she expects to work late tomorrow and admits to being home roughly two hours later than normal, would you believe the claim? Do you doubt it, with or without reasonable cause? Perhaps you are willing to trust your partner's claim, but only after fact-checking your partner in some way, like using a Find My Phone app to see if your partner's phone is still at the workplace. If you choose to doubt or need evidence that shows your partner is honest, then you have a trust issue on your hands.

Another symptom you may be suffering from is always expecting the worst in others. When you are suspicious that you will be betrayed at any moment, you will find it difficult to discern whether your partner's motives are genuine or sinister despite never having reason to doubt your partner's intentions. This often stems from someone taking advantage of your trust in the past and leaves you feeling unable to trust anyone. If you find yourself second-guessing whether your partner is genuine, then you have an issue with trusting others.

This often leads to another symptom of trust issues, which is keeping everyone at a distance, including your partner. Despite how much you may want to develop a deep, meaningful, and secure relationship with someone, your trust issues may be causing a stark disconnection with everyone around you. This can show how you view your friendships and relationships.

If you feel either is superficial, then your trust issues have you struggling to develop a connection with others. This makes it difficult for you to be vulnerable around the people you would normally feel safest around, which can then manifest in your emotional and physical intimacy with others. Your lack of vulnerability may make you feel like an outcast among your friends. Or alone, even in the company of your partner.

Emotionally, you may feel guarded and unwilling to let others know whether you are uncomfortable or pleased about something because you do not trust them to be mindful of your feelings. Physically, you may prove uncomfortable with being touched platonically or sexually and often react by stiffening or flinching away. If these examples sound like what you are doing, then your trust issue is real and must be addressed before you can have that fulfilling relationship part of you may crave.

Trust Building Exercises for Couples

Overcoming trust issues is difficult and messy. There is no getting around how challenging this will be for you and your partner, but it must be done to make the relationship work. Learning to trust despite having valleys filled with trust issues is an accomplishment to be proud of, so reassure your partner of your pride in their efforts. It will be an emotionally demanding and exhausting process for your partner, but having you help him or her will make the process easier and worth it.

A safe start to building trust together is by stating what you plan to do, then doing it. It may seem simple and strange for an exercise, but it is effective. By letting each other know your plans and then following through with them, you show that you can be trusted to stay on task and take care of business. This allows your partner to see that you mean what you say and will slowly ease their mistrust.

This practice also opens the way to honest communication, which may be something your partner desperately needs to practice. When handling trust issues, communication will be vital in showing your partner how serious you take the relationship and his or her feelings. This also means not holding back with any news, good or bad. That level of honesty can be hurtful when bad, but will ultimately relieve your partner's trust issues. This is because you chose not to hide anything from your partner, and that vulnerability is something your partner also needs.

So, if mistakes were made, do not sugarcoat them or try to dance around the situation. Let it lay bare between you two, so it can be appropriately addressed. It may be difficult at first because your partner may prove sensitive to bad news in the beginning, but that will change as your partner adjusts to the openness about mistakes.

Conversations like this will further bolster your partner's confidence in you and the relationship. It shows you have integrity. By demonstrating your moral principles and providing full disclosure about what is happening between you and your partner, you are further easing your partner's worries because you are providing evidence for your partner to count on during times of distress. These moments can then be used by your partner to help prevent him or her from jumping to irrational conclusions in the future.

Solo Trust Building Exercises

As important as it can be to work with your partner to assuage trust issues, certain tasks must be done alone to further alleviate the pain of past betrayals. For one, you must accept that trust is earned and given. Just because someone wronged you in the past does not mean every new person you meet will do the same. The person who wronged you is the one you no longer trust, and that is reasonable. But to put that altered view on your current partner who has done nothing to incite your doubt is selfish.

To help differentiate between past and present, practice recognizing when your partner does something that should earn your trust. This exercise helps you craft a new, more accurate opinion of your partner instead of relying on the assumptions that your trust issues originally led you to believe. By pointing out these trustworthy actions, you constantly challenge the perception of mistrust and allow yourself the chance to develop genuine connections with your partner. Before starting this exercise, start listing what you believe are acts of trust so you can begin recognizing them in action.

Alongside this exercise, also consider sorting between people who hurt you and those who did not. Trust issues have a cruel effect that blurs the picture to make you believe everyone is the same. This belief is blatantly false and must be challenged. Practice recognizing your partner as unrelated to your past hurts. Your partner is his or her person, and the source of your trust issues is another person entirely.

It may help to write down the differences to help sort your thoughts. You could fill a section of a book or dedicate pages in your digital notes to separate people and use these notes to sort out who is related to what incident. When someone betrays your trust in some way, adjust that person's notes accordingly and do not tamper with anyone else's. This will help you realize that Person A has done something wrong, but Person B has not, so Person B is still trustworthy.

Finally, take time to identify when your trust issues flare worse than usual. For example, if your partner returning home late from work causes your trust issues to feed your negative thoughts, then you must find a means to mitigate the flares. Having your partner send you a text or call you to warn you about the change in plans might help. This also provides you the opportunity to give him or her an excuse that you are comfortable with, like asking your partner to pick up dinner on the way back or run to the store for something. This way, you have your partner's acceptable reason for being late, and you have soothed your nerves because you provided a reason for your partner to be away a bit longer than usual.

You can also practice distracting yourself when you know unease and mistrust are starting to flare. Find something that requires your full concentration to accomplish. When you have no room to let your imagination wander, your anxiety and mistrust will be unable to cause a riot in your mind and relationship. Identifying the situations and rerouting your nervous energy are effective ways to reduce the stress caused by trust issues.

CHAPTER 7
Forgiving Yourself For Feeling Anxiety

Jake's relationship with Anna has been rocky, but somehow, they have managed to keep it together. Jake blames himself for the hardships they endured. If only he was not so weak-willed or hopeless. Were he better at speaking his mind, then Anna would know what he was struggling with and why he was always so quick to apologize; his anxieties do not approve of speaking his mind.

He knows he can do better and recognizes he should be better, but it feels impossible. Every mistake is another reason why he should give up and let Anna go. She would be happier without his screw ups and deserved someone more capable. Someone more confident. His internal struggle worsens every day and makes it harder to go even a day without slipping up in some way. Slowly, Jake's anxieties take over until, finally, Anna pulls him close.

"I forgive you," she explains as she hugs her boyfriend tight. "But I see that is not enough." Jake is silent as he shakily clings to Anna. Is this it, then? Was this the final straw? "You need to forgive yourself, too. It is not fair for you to forgive me so easily when I do something wrong, but condemn yourself for the same mistake."

"I don't do that," is his weak protest, but even as he says it, it rings false even in his ears. "I just... I don't..." He has nothing more to say on the matter. Anything else would be an excuse or a lie, so his lips tighten close, and he shrinks into himself. What a useless person he is, being unable to say anything.

"You have to forgive yourself." Anna softly repeats this as she rubs soothing circles on Jake's back. "It is okay to feel bad and regret what you did, but please. Do not let it eat you up like this." There is no response. After a moment of silence, she pulls back a bit so she can meet Jake's gaze.

"Will you make it up to me, then?" She waits for Jake to process the question, then smiles as confusion colors his brown eyes. "Will you practice self-forgiveness with me?"

He does not understand what Anna means by that, but he also has no reason to refuse. If this means Anna will not be mad, then Jake would do this a thousand times to show his remorse. Unable to trust his voice, Jake merely nods in agreement. Anna's smile widens into a relieved grin. Jake's lessons on how to forgive himself begins.

His anxieties are still on high alert, but they do not bother him as much after the lessons. Jake never notices it, but his smile becomes more genuine as his shoulders relax. Anna continues to monitor his progress with learning to forgive, and as they work on this, the hardships in their relationship lessen. They live happily and feel secure together.

The Importance of Forgiving Yourself

Anna works hard with Jake to teach him the importance of self-forgiveness. In the beginning, Jake did not understand what that meant and why Anna cared so much about it, but he learned how much good could come from it. So, what then, is self-forgiveness? The definition depends on the person asked. But the consensus is this: Self-forgiveness is the ability to accept the disruptive behavior or action for what it was. To not dwell on what has happened because it is in the past, and to move on to do better.

Everyone knows how to forgive and let go when someone else makes a mistake, but it is difficult to apply that same level of mindfulness with yourself. It is normal to feel bad and wish to right any wrongs you made, but it is not healthy to dwell on the mistakes. Beating yourself up over the mistake and always using the mistake against yourself is not healthy. Just as your friend would forgive you for spilling soda on the couch, you must forgive yourself for the mistake, too.

Just as your partner forgives you for assuming the worst about how late your partner returned home due to your anxiety, you must also forgive yourself for assuming the worst. There will be times when your anxiety overcomes your rational thinking. It will happen, and there is little we can do about it.

Reflecting, acknowledging, and forgiving yourself for feeling strongly is healthy. Self-forgiveness allows you to move on and learn from the mistake. If you dwell on it and refuse to forgive yourself despite others having already done so, then you are forcing yourself to remain stagnant and trapping yourself in the past. This prevents you from being the best you can be while giving your anxiety more fuel to use against you.

By failing or refusing to forgive yourself for your actions, reactions, and suffering, you will worsen your mental health with greater stress and self-directed resentment. A consequence of this includes further reducing your self-esteem and the potential of promoting depression or other related issues. This causes you to fixate on your difficult emotions and gives more control to your anxiety.

The longer you ruminate on how poorly you handled your anxiety, the worse your anxiety may become. As you feel your anxieties grow stronger and more active, your ability to forgive yourself will further decrease, and you will find yourself in a perpetual state of frustration, stress, remorse, and helplessness as everything spirals seemingly out of control. By learning to forgive and move on, you allow yourself to let go of the mistake and say, "Yes, how I acted or reacted is wrong. I can and will do better."

This is not to say you should brush off and forget about any mistakes you make. Forgiving yourself does not mean ignoring the fact that you reacted poorly to a situation or that your anxiety got the better of you.

Self-forgiveness is meant to make it easier for you to disconnect from the situation in a way that allows you to acknowledge what happened, why, and how to do better.

It forces us to acknowledge that we are being overly critical about ourselves and our anxieties, but that is not to say being self-critical is wrong. We are critical of ourselves to better ourselves so we may live happier, fulfilling lives. It can be difficult to stop internalizing your flaws and failures. But by trying, you open yourself to easing the stress and reducing the likelihood of certain situations and accidents triggering anxiety flares.

The Relationship Between Forgiveness and Anxiety

When you suffer from anxiety, it is hard to forget or ignore it. You always feel it nearby, sitting in the back of your mind as it waits for you to drop your guard and let it move upfront. When this happens, it is easy to fall victim and let it run its course. By the time you regain your rational thoughts, the damage has been done, and you are faced with the results. Maybe you have hurt your partner's feelings with the unreasonable accusations your anxiety spat. Or perhaps you upset your partner because you did not want him or her to go out without you and effectively canceled all of your partner's plans. Whatever may have happened, your anxiety will have caused serious damage at the time. Your partner would have forgiven you, though it may not have been easy because you might have been particularly harmful in your anxious state, would you have forgiven yourself?

Most people would have dwelled on how badly they acted and clammed up upon realizing how out-of-line they acted. A lot of people would have berated themselves for acting so selfishly, being so foolish, and slung around other self-derogatory remarks over the behavior. Very few people would have looked at what they did, acknowledged that it was fueled by their anxiety, and chose not to drown in everything that went wrong.

The practice of looking back is called self-reflection, which is a powerful tool when learning to forgive yourself and others. But, as mentioned above, dwelling on the issues does not help. This is ruminating, which is a spiral of negative thoughts that will ultimately harm your mental health and health of your relationship. Ruminating causes you to forget about any good qualities of the situation or yourself and traps you in the negative mindset that fuels your anxiety.

Benefits of Choosing Forgiveness

By choosing to forgive yourself for how your anxiety flares, you are acknowledging that anxiety is part of life, and it cannot always be controlled. This also allows you the opportunity to address what caused your anxiety so you may reflect and learn how to handle the situation in the future better. Choosing forgiveness also makes way for other benefits, as discovered by medical professionals–including cognitive-behavioral therapists–in studies concerning how holding self-resentment or ruminating agitate anxiety and stress.

The first and obvious benefits include reduced anxiety symptoms and blood pressure. You also reaffirm positive relationships with your partner, friends, and family by choosing forgiveness over self-resentment. Practicing self-forgiveness has been proven to improve your mental and emotional health, both of which can reduce the severity of your anxiety.

You may also find your productivity levels increasing due to practicing self-forgiveness. This is because of the positive acceptance of what has happened and acknowledgment that you will do better to stop you from hyper-focusing on how everything can-and-will go wrong. When you are not exaggerating the negatives your anxiety has caused, you allow yourself to move on and tend to important needs or goals.

The Art of Forgiving Yourself

When learning to forgive yourself, the belief that you are unworthy of it or that you are letting yourself off easy can be cruel and demoralizing. Thoughts like this stem from your anxiety and other insecurities, so do not let them stop you from improving yourself with forgiveness. Such self-judgment and blame have no place in your life. If you were truly unworthy of forgiveness, then your partner would not be forgiving. If you were letting yourself off easy, then you would not feel such remorse for what your anxiety has caused.

Acknowledge that these thoughts are real and deserve their fair consideration, but do not blind yourself from the facts. It is fine and normal to be upset with yourself, but do not let it eat at you forever. By changing your behavior to allow self-forgiveness, you will find yourself more motivated to change and less likely to repeat past mistakes. By acknowledging the concerns and thoughts introduced by your anxiety, you are practicing self-awareness.

This practice is a strong first step to learning how to forgive yourself. This awareness is meant to push you in the direction of accepting your anxiety and its consequences without judgment. During those times, when you feel you are irredeemable because your anxiety is so difficult to live with, be sure to question the fairness of your thoughts. Are you especially frustrated because your anxiety has flared again? Do you honestly believe you are such a terrible person because you have anxiety?

When practicing self-awareness, bear in mind that you are human. That old saying, "Everyone makes mistakes" is tried and true. Though not everyone suffers from anxiety, that does not mean such people have never been upset and unwilling to forgive themselves for their overreactions. As we grow up, we are taught that failing is part of life, and that getting back up is always what follows. It is okay to cry or be upset when you fall, so long as you remember to get up and keep going.

Instead of criticizing yourself for often falling due to anxiety, forgive yourself for falling. Sometimes, our anxiety gets the best of us. It happens, and it will continue to happen despite our best efforts.

When it happens, remember to be kind to yourself. Berating yourself will only worsen your mood, deepen your stress, and give power to your anxiety. Instead of growing agitated, ask yourself if you are now okay. If you are feeling emotionally compromised, then take the time you need to soothe your nerves. Ask yourself what you need right that second, and if it is something easy to accomplish, take care of that need.

Sorting out your feelings and needs will help you come to terms with what your anxiety has caused. Once soothed, rectify the mistakes and learn from them. You can look at the problem, analyze the result, and find a way to prevent it from escalating a second time. The action you take is crucial to allowing yourself self-forgiveness. By acting and making things right, you give yourself the opening you may not have realized you needed to forgive yourself.

You also open yourself to empathizing with your partner when you forgive yourself. When you do not allow yourself to self-forgive, you stop yourself from seeing the effects of your actions and reaction on others. Yes, you may understand that you hurt your partner with your anxiety flare and internalized that as another reason why you do not deserve forgiveness, but you also keep a narrow mind by seeing only the momentary hurt you caused your partner.

You do not empathize with your partner by seeing only how you hurt them. This alienates your partner's feelings and opinions because part of you refuses to accept how your partner already forgave you for what happened, instead of empathizing with your partner. You keep your partner a victim in your mind, and that is a disservice to both of you. By committing to the practice of self-forgiveness, you allow your partner's thoughts and opinions to wash over you and be fully addressed instead of selectively addressed.

Like this, you can tell yourself, "I learned from this. I did what I could to fix it. I am proud and forgive myself for what happened." Choosing to practice self-forgiveness is a slow process that may feel pointless in the beginning, but it is effective. Commit to it and watch as you and your partner achieve greater happiness, communication, and understanding in your relationship.

Anxiety Is a Part of Life

Anxiety makes relationships difficult to manage, not to mention your everyday life, but that does not mean you should be ashamed, embarrassed, or upset about struggling with it. According to the Anxiety and Depression Association of America (ADAA), anxiety has become part of life for many of us. In the United States alone, it was recorded that over 40 million individuals from age 18 years old and up suffer from anxiety disorders. As for children, it has been recorded that roughly 25.1% of children aged 13 to 18 years old suffer from anxiety disorders.

That is how common anxiety has become over the years, but that accounts for only the United States. Globally, the World Health Organization (WHO) has revealed statistics stating 1 in 13 globally is suffering from anxiety. This makes anxiety among the most common mental disorders in the world. Anxiety is also closely tied with other disorders, including depression and eating disorders.

Despite anxiety becoming commonplace globally, it is technically a treatable condition. Less than 40% of the affected American population opts to get treated for anxiety for various reasons. 25% or less of the affected global population opts for treatment, too. Due to how common anxiety has become around the world, online and in-person sources have begun quoting misinformation and myths about ways to address your anxiety.

One such popular misconception is how the medication for anxiety is supposedly addictive, so people should take medication only if desperate or unable to resist the disorders. This has been repeatedly proven false by medical professionals, but popular beliefs are quicker to spread. Technically, antidepressants are not addictive, but it has been acknowledged that repeated intake can lead to greater tolerance. This has caused the illusion of users becoming addicted.

Another popular illusion about medication is the belief that medication is the sole means of treating anxiety disorders. Contrary to this claim, it is acknowledged that medication is an effective method for treating anxiety. Still, therapy for cognitive behavior (CBT) is equally effective for most and more effective for many. The combination of medication and CBT has also proven particularly effective in the long run.

A particularly cruel myth that is meant to help control your negative thinking is snapping a rubber band on your wrist. You are supposed to do this whenever you feel your thoughts starting to spiral or when you feel your anxiety starting to act up. This is self-harm and does not help your situation.

The very idea of trying to suppress your emotions, thoughts, and anxiety is incorrect and extremely harmful. Instead of reducing your anxiety, you are making it stronger and persistent. The ADAA also warns that trying to suppress your anxiety makes your anxiety flare more frequently. If you choose to make use of the rubber band myth, then you will force yourself into a vicious cycle of frequent anxiety attacks with no signs of it easing.

Other myths include avoiding feeling stressed and situations that can be considered stressful; living a healthy lifestyle and avoiding caffeine makes the anxiety go away, and receiving endless reassurances and assistance to dodge stressful situations help with anxiety. All of the above have no factual basis and have repeatedly been proven incorrect. Like the other myths, however, these beliefs are commonly spread and have unnecessarily harmed affected individuals, all of whom do not deserve to be fed such misinformation.

They believe that avoiding stress and potentially stressful situations is insulting and results in the affected individuals being treated like young children. Stress is part of life and is often unavoidable. It is demoralizing to lose your freedom and be treated like your entire being is fragile. The belief that avoiding it also further enforces your anxiety, making it a more permanent fixture in your life. Furthermore, you will never learn to overcome the anxiety if you avoid the problem, leaving you permanently anxious about whatever causes it.

The claim about living a healthier lifestyle and avoiding caffeine can help reduce stress and consequently ease your anxiety, but it does not banish your problems. Anxiety disorders are present in even the healthiest individuals, and though stress can cause your anxiety to flare more, the stress itself is never the cause of your anxiety in the first place. It is great to live healthier lives and to consume less caffeine, but the struggle with anxiety is mental, not physical, so changing your lifestyle will require you to change how you behave, feel, think, or address difficult situations.

Then there is the endless supply of reassurances from family and friends. As well-meaning as their actions may be, they are technically inhibiting you from growing and overcoming your anxiety by trying to protect you. Their insistence on taking care of anything that can cause you distress means you will never have the chance to face your anxiety and tame it. The more you avoid, the more permanent the anxiety becomes in your life. If your family and friends want to be genuine help, then supporting and encouraging you to address your anxieties and insecurities are the steps they should take.

Finally, another common misunderstanding of anxiety is the belief that nothing can be done for certain people because these people are not suffering from anxiety. According to this belief, these people are just neurotic or natural worrywarts. People like this are helpless, according to the myth.

The truth revealed by medical professionals is that even neurotic and worrywart individuals can be helped. Like other disorders, therapy is a solid means of helping reduce anxiety, stress, and worry. Your temperament and how long you have lived with such habits or disorders does not change the fact that therapy can help you regain control of your life.

Helpful Resources When Struggling with Anxiety

Addressing your anxiety and finding ways to soothe its effects is difficult. As stated previously, numerous sources are claiming to have quick fixes that are guaranteed to cure you of your anxiety. But there is no such thing as curing your anxiety with a "quick and easy fix." That simply does not exist and is often a hoax to get money out of you.

If you choose to search for legitimate resources, always check for credentials. Look specifically for information stating the information is from certified therapists who specialize in cognitive behaviors. Find the biographies of the authors if you must and search for mentions of academic degrees, professional certifications and licenses, and other pieces of evidence that prove their experience is real.

A solid source for effective and reliable means of overcoming your anxiety is the ADAA. The resources cited and provided through this organization include treatment options, contacts, and webinars, where specialists address concerns about anxiety disorders and related insecurities. The ADAA also has resources to help you determine what fantastical claims are nonsense and what online sources are scams to take advantage of your anxiety.

Another good place to start is the National Institute of Mental Health (NIMH). This is an organization that researches mental disorders. The organization is dedicated to helping everyone understand that mental illnesses are real. It also participates in research for treating mental illnesses. NIMH is determined to help those of us suffering from mental disorders like anxiety by offering means to prevent, recover, and cure such struggles.

The Substance Abuse and Mental Health Services Administration (SAMHSA) also has resources to help with mental disorders like anxiety. This is an agency within the U.S. government meant to assist the public in matters of behavioral health. Speaking with members of SAMHSA is completely free, confidential, and open all year, every day.

CHAPTER 8
Improving Communication With Your Partner

Kacey and her boyfriend, Jeremy, are visibly nervous as they sit across from each other at the dining table. They both have a lot to say about each other, themselves, and the relationship. It is hard to speak up despite how much they want to share their thoughts. Finally, Jeremy bites the bullet and speaks up.

"I no longer feel comfortable," Jeremy blurts out, then pauses. "I-In our relationship." He adds, as if uncertain whether his intention was clear.

"Well, I cannot say I am too happy in our relationship." Kacey does not mean to sound bitter. When she registers the hurt in her boyfriend's eyes, however, she quickly amends with, "Lately, that is. I am restless to take things to the next step, but you always dodge the subject when I bring it up, and that upsets me."

Finally, they find themselves able to lay things out as their grievances escape them in the momentum of their accidental confessions. It grows easier to explain the problems and insecurities they have kept quiet about, and once everything is said, they stare at each other with uncertainty. There is a sense of relief in the air as they consider the other. Still, this is unfamiliar territory for them both, so the silence lingers longer than necessary.

"I do not want to pressure you," offers Kacey after a long moment. When Jeremy tilts his head a bit to show he is listening, she continues after a deep breath. "I just want to know why you will not talk things out with me. About moving forward with our relationship. Is that part of why you are uncomfortable?"

"It is." His confession is soft, and almost sounds mournful. He does not feel ready to move forward in their relationship for several reasons, a few of which he admits aloud. Though they are compatible, and Kacey has been great for him, he worries about his contribution to the relationship. When Kacey first brought up the idea of moving forward, Jeremy reflected on the relationship and decided he was not trying hard enough for the relationship to warrant moving forward. He wished to improve so he could stand with Kacey on the idea of moving forward, not hold her back because he is constantly two steps behind.

After a few minutes of allowing Jeremy to explain himself and his insecurities about his place in their relationship, Kacey speaks. She reassures her boyfriend about all he has done that has improved their relationship. He has helped her through the days, and how much she appreciates him. It is not easy to get through to him, but Kacey does her best. She asks Jeremy to see things through her eyes and reminds him of the lessons she learned since starting this relationship. They are good for each other; they take care of each other. Their relationship is secure.

In this example, the two have practiced the most important exercise for a couple: Honest communication. The ability to be vulnerable and speak honestly, intimately, with your partner in a relationship is arguably the most important factor in determining whether the relationship is healthy and secure. If you find it difficult to open to your partner about what troubles you, then you cannot honestly say that you feel secure in your relationship.

If you felt genuinely secure, you would trust your partner with your vulnerabilities. That is not to say you may believe you feel secure. A certain part of you may be entirely comfortable with the relationship, and that part may be what you point to when you claim to feel secure. This is a mild act of denial and selective focus. By choosing to focus on just the part of you that feels secure, you neglect to care for everything else that makes you.

Neglecting everything else that is unhappy or uncertain is a choice made from anxiety or insecurity. It is unhealthy and will change as you work to overcome the struggles which hold you back. Choosing to address everything that makes you unhappy will further improve your chances of standing above your anxieties and insecurities. So do not pretend that the entire relationship is wonderful when you are not able to fully communicate your fears and needs.

How Communication Looks: The Good and Bad

Bear in mind; the ability to communicate is not solely reliant on you. Your partner must be willing to sit with you and contribute to the conversation, too. It is near impossible to overcome conflict when only one side is willing to talk it out, so if you find your partner intentionally or unintentionally failing to contribute, make sure this becomes a priority topic.

Relationships that struggle to hold intimate and supportive communication are ones that have the most conflict. They are also the ones to break down and leave the two parties weighed down with unnecessary baggage after parting ways. Poor communication comes in many forms.

You know you or your partner struggles with communication if either of you chooses not to dedicate full attention to the serious conversation. Arguments that stem from attempts to hold important conversations also point to poor communication because one of you feels attacked, and that feeling often leaves a person defensive or unresponsive to the matter. A major sign of poor communication is your level of self-esteem or confidence. When you do not feel anything comes out of talking with your partner, communication becomes less important because you feel incapable of getting your point across.

None of this is healthy in a relationship. Proper, healthy communication is filled with trust that the other will not scorn or dismiss you. It is formed by the necessary honesty to ensure you are both on the same page on matters to prevent further conflict. Above all, it is formed on mutual respect, because you are both upstanding individuals who are in love and appreciate the importance of each other's thoughts and feelings.

When your relationship has healthy communication, you should feel every talk is productive, that your partner genuinely cares about the issues you want to address, and that your partner supports you in a way that promotes positive reinforcement to the relationship. Among the most crucial aspects of healthy communication is how well you both listen to each other.

Your ability to sit and listen to your partner's grievances without interrupting is crucial to ensuring your partner feels secure about telling you what is on his or her mind. The same goes for the reverse–if your partner interrupts you often with snide or annoying comments, your confidence on how well this conversation goes will plummet. Be polite, listen to each other, and seriously consider where the other is coming from with this matter. Putting aside your thoughts to better understand your partner's frustrations and needs will make your partner feel heard and better appreciated.

You may feel there is no problem with leaving dirty dishes in the sink for a day or two in a row. But seeing those dishes may stress your partner because it is a reminder that he or she was treated as more of a maid than a lover in a previous relationship. Be empathetic–that is, acknowledge your partner's pain and think about how you would feel in his or her position about the situation. Yes, your partner knows you do not think of him or her as your maid, but sometimes your partner feels that way because of the dishes.

Healthy Communication in Action

In a secure relationship, healthy communication becomes a regular part of life. You will find yourself actively looking to avoid unnecessary misunderstandings in a conversation, and at times, you may find yourself bringing up previous conversations to further clarify points for various reasons. For Kacey and Jeremy, their form of communication often has them returning to conversations from minutes, hours, even days earlier. This is because one of them realized how something said may have come off with the wrong intention. It is normal to return to previous conversations like this, so it is recommended you normalize this in your relationship, too. Misunderstandings happen often, and though they do not always cause anger or hurt, they can cause confusion or misdirection. You want to normalize revisiting conversation for several reasons.

First, you will not always get your thoughts and feelings perfectly explained in one attempt. Your communication will not be perfect every time you sit down. It is best to accept that there will be times when you or your partner will want to come back to old conversations.

Also, when sitting down to hold a serious conversation, it is normal for only one of you to be fully aware of what will be discussed. Because of this, only one of you will be emotionally ready for what will be said. If you were the one to start the conversation, you already know how you are affected by the issues. And have sorted your feelings on the matter. In that scenario, your partner will be in a position of listening, absorbing, and sorting his or her feelings. By normalizing the option to return to previous conversations, you allow your partner the ability to fully sort his or her emotions and come back to the topic prepared.

Another healthy act from Kacey's and Jeremey's example of communication is found in Kacey's response to Jeremy's confessed worries. She acknowledged how inadequate Jeremy felt in the relationship, then reminded him how much he brings to the relationship. This is an example of sharing positive feelings when communicating.

When you share positive feelings, you remind your partner how important he or she is to you, and that you appreciate how hard your partner tries in the relationship. It may not be perfect, and mistakes may be made at times, but the intent to do better and to make everything work is what matters. Anxious individuals may need to be reminded how you admire how hard they try to make things work, but remember that even an anxious person's partner can benefit from such positive reminders.

Improving Communication in Your Relationship

Improving communication in your relationship is a goal you both must share. It will do you no good if you put in the effort to do better, but your partner continues to dodge the seriousness of the conversation. Before practicing effective communication, insist your partner try this with you. In a secure relationship, your partner should be willing to participate, though it is expected for him or her to be hesitant if your partner is an anxious person. Encourage and praise your partner for trying and remind him or her that this is a new experience for you both. Knowing that you are both new can ease your partner's nerves because it is clear neither of you will be upset with the other for making mistakes.

Once you are both on board with practicing effective communication, the first step to take is establishing a time to communicate. When you or your partner are bothered or stressed, it is best to hold the important conversation at a time when neither of you will be swayed by emotion or distracted by other obligations. Choose a time when you are both available, calm, and not distracted. You will find your ability to communicate is better when you are both fully engaged because you are both free to talk.

Choosing the right time to talk also means not holding serious conversations over text or a phone call. These conversations are best-handled face-to-face, in a situation where you can see the other's expressions, body language, and gauge the other's attention. It is fine to write your thoughts down to better sort them for presentation, but do not send your thoughts in a text for your partner to interpret. This gives your partner the freedom to read between the lines and find nonexistent connotations to your words.

It is too easy to interpret the text in tones based on our personal feelings. If your partner is at work and stressed or displeased with how the day is going, a text or email from you about something serious may be colored with negativity. It is colored with negativity because your partner was already in a mood before your message. There is a greater chance of your partner feeling like he or she is being attacked on top of a bad day at work. Which will lead to worse miscommunication and greater complications in the relationship.

Even in-person, sounding harsh, and using certain words can still forge the illusion of you attacking your partner in the conversation. Resist using the word "you" when trying to communicate displeasure about a situation. That word places all blame on your partner and can be considered an attack and unnecessary criticism. Instead, use "I" and "we" more often to show that you are a team and that you are not blaming your partner for what is happening.

When discussing the matter at hand, focus solely on your thoughts, feelings, and reactions. You cannot know what your partner thinks or feels on the matter, so criticizing or blaming your partner for his or her reactions is cruel and undermines your message. This conversation should be about revealing yourself to your partner. This includes your irrational feelings and thoughts, both of which should always be addressed.

That does not mean to victimize or indirectly accuse your partner of your irrational feelings. So, if you feel hurt or disappointed, refrain from claiming that you should not feel hurt or disappointed. You both know you should not feel this way or that, but the fact of the matter is that you do. Dancing around the truth that you do feel this way is meaningless and does not help you nor your partner. Acknowledging these feelings allows both parties to understand better how deeply the situation cut you.

Furthermore, you must both give up the need to be right about the situation. There are two stories to this situation: Yours *and* your partner's. There is a grey area where the stories meet, so focus on that grey area while expressing your thoughts and feelings on the matter. You both are affected by the situation, so remember to listen and acknowledge your partner's perspective. You may be surprised to realize how differently you two view the subject.

Finally, the best way to improve communication in your relationship is resolving the conflict without letting anger cloud your judgment. If you feel your emotions or temper running high, or see your partner is getting upset, stop the conversation. Meaningless words you both will regret can slip out if your emotions run too high, so stop to take a breath. Inform your partner that you need to pause the conversation so you can both get back into the right mindset for it.

Again, it is perfectly normal to come back to a previous conversation, so normalize this in your relationship. Take the necessary time to cool off, then come back and see if your partner is also ready to try again. Allow yourself a moment to think about what was said, how it may have sounded. What more needs to be said and what needs to be clarified to remedy the situation. Realize that your non-verbal cues may have escalated the conversation, then work on maintaining calmer cues, so emotions do not run high again.

Non-Verbal Communication in Your Relationship

In the effort to improve communication in your relationship, first, consider your non-verbal communication. It is important to improve your non-verbal communication before practicing the verbal component. Your non-verbal cues include your posture when speaking or listening, the tone of your voice when explaining yourself or the situation, and the expressions you make when speaking or listening.

Our non-verbal cues are often forgotten when approaching each other for an important conversation. We can have our entire speech planned to clearly explain why something is an issue and how it felt, but our non-verbal cues may give the wrong impression. This is a common mistake that requires practice to overcome.

For example, if your posture is stiff or has you leaning forward, you can appear furious and aggressive. This can cause your partner to shrink back, become defensive, or refrain from responding to protect him- or herself. If you have a habit of wild gesturing, your partner may grow fearful of saying the wrong thing and refuse to speak because he or she does not want to risk being smacked.

Your tone of voice can also lead to unintended misunderstandings. If you sound angry about the situation despite feeling hurt, your partner will believe your tone as your true emotions. Your volume will also betray your intentions. When too loud, aggressive tones like anger will feel more emphasized. When too quiet, your partner may be unable to hear you and misinterpret your words based on guesses of what you said.

Finally, your expression. For many of us, it is difficult to school our faces to remain steady with a neutral expression. Because of this, it can be expected to find yourself struggling to maintain a civil conversation when you are upset, for your expression may give you an air of aggression like your tone or body posture. The combination of the three makes any conversation difficult. Therefore, you should take the necessary time to practice your non-verbal communication.

There are steps you can take to ensure you do not come off threatening or irritated. One such step includes taking a seat even if your partner is standing. On a subconscious level, this reassures your partner that you have no intention of getting physical and allows your partner to control the distance. This can be reassuring and give your partner comfort.

You should also avoid closing off your body position because a closed position is viewed more defensively or displeased. Examples of an open body position include not crossing your arms or legs. Having your arms relaxed at your sides shows you are open to your partner's opinions and are willing to compromise to make both sides happy. This is to also stop you from fidgeting. Which is a habit that distracts both of you from the matter at hand. Fidgeting has a negative connotation of being nervous or bored in a situation, so take measures to avoid this, so your partner does not think you are disinterested in the conversation.

As for your legs, having your legs relaxed side-by-side shows you are interested in having this conversation. This shows that you are ready to listen, consider your partner's thoughts, and ready to engage in the conversation. This is especially important if your partner chooses to sit, too. In such a case, you can angle yourself toward your partner to give a friendly and inviting air to ease the tension of the serious conversation. Sitting at an angle while keeping your legs, uncrossed shows that you are non confrontational, which will ease your partner's anxieties or insecurities if they suffer from such conditions.

A final show of non-verbal communication to practice is silently acknowledging your partner as he or she speaks. Subtle nods to show you are listening is an example of silent acknowledgment. This encourages your partner to continue with any previously withheld grievances until it is all revealed. When you reply, ensure you repeat or verbally acknowledge parts of your partner's speech to emphasize that you listened and understood what was being shared.

CONCLUSION

Thank you for making it through to the end of *Anxiety in a Relationship*, let's hope it was informative and able to provide you with all of the tools you need to achieve your goals, whatever they may be. It takes great courage to choose to fight against anxieties so you can strengthen your relationship, so take pride that you have completed this book with the intent to conquer such hardships.

To recap, you have successfully read about the ups and downs of dealing with various anxieties in a relationship. As you went along, you read about solutions that can help ease the anxieties, not completely banish them, because such thoughts and disorders cannot be simply willed away. They are like our inner demons: They will always be with us to haunt and tempt us back into old habits.

Remember, your bravery and desire to confront your anxieties, whatever they may be, is admirable and inspiring. You have chosen to look your anxieties in the face and tell them, "I am greater than you, and I can prove it." You are right and should be proud of your efforts to improve yourself.

As you read through the book, hopefully, you have found certain solutions helpful or inspiring for how to overcome the anxieties or insecurities you feel in your relationship. Do not feel discouraged if you feel the need to go back and read through a few chapters, though. There was a lot of information to take in, so it only makes sense to go back once or twice to better absorb what you read.

If you do choose to reread certain sections, I encourage you to invite your partner to join you in your readings. It may help further cement your dedication to improving the relationship and show your partner how serious such anxieties can be for those of us who suffer from them. The examples shared in the related chapters make for good sources of discussion, too. Try to draw your partner into discussing any similarities you may have noticed in your relationship. This way, your partner will start to see the parallels, and the information will sink in better.

As you and your partner come to a better understanding of the anxieties affecting your relationship, the next step will be to address them together. As you saw, certain anxieties will require you to practice exercises on your own, but do not worry. Your partner can support these efforts with gentle reminders and practice them with him- or herself, too.

Once again, I recognize that this is one book in thousands on the subject. Because of this, I thank you for taking the time out of your day to give this book a read during your journey of learning, acceptance, and teamwork. I wish you the best with overcoming your anxieties and making your relationship healthy and secure.

Finally, if you found this book useful in any way, then leaving a review on Amazon is always appreciated!

DESCRIPTION

The time to let go of your anxieties and insecurities to enjoy your loving, secure relationship has come. We all have our shortcomings and wish to experience the full joy of loving and being loved. Unfortunately, anxiety is a cruel master or mistress who does not approve of any relationship. But you do not have to suffer under such cruelty.

You deserve the happiness of experiencing that stable relationship you have found. You deserve to enjoy the fulfillment you experience with your partner. Anxiety has no place in your relationship. If you have found it nestled in your relationship and want it gone, then read on because you will learn and practice exercises that tackle the root causes of anxiety.

You can expect to learn about the following:

- How to recognize the telltale signs of anxiety in you or your partner, as well as learn the deeper meaning of each sign. Expect to evaluate your own relationship every step of the way so you can determine what struggles your relationship faces and what must be done to overcome them.
- How to recognize negative thoughts caused by anxiety. You will come to understand that such thoughts are formed by habit, and habits can be broken. You will learn and practice exercises to dismiss such thoughts to better yourself and your relationship.
- Discover the many insecurities we all can face, recognize what all affects your relationship, and learn how to banish them. You will also learn to recognize insecurities your partner struggles with and help them grow alongside you.
- How to love yourself despite the struggles you face. You will undergo the transformation of recognizing what your partner loves about you and realize that you, too, love these aspects about yourself. This lesson will further improve your ability to love your partner and embrace the secure relationship you share.
- Strategies to help you let go of what cannot be controlled and focus on what is within your power. You will realize that life happens, the good and bad, whether we want it or not. Lessons on how to forgive and let go will improve your self-esteem and your confidence in the relationship's longevity.
- And so much more, like overcoming trust issues and improving communication between you and your partner!

If you are single because you fear your anxieties are a hindrance to creating meaningful and deep connections with others, then you can expect to gain the confidence you desire from reading on. Relationships can be intimidating because of anxiety, but that will change. The lessons and exercises provided in this book are applicable to more than romantic relationships, so rest assured that you are not limited in your life.

You are not beholden to your anxiety, and it is time it realized this. There is no need to hesitate with this book in hand. You are equipped to sit your anxiety down and have the conversation that ends it all. From this moment on, you can confidently look your anxiety in the eye and tell it, "This is it! I am breaking up with Anxiety!"

Make your anxiety pack its bags and show it to the door because you are making room for relationships that will benefit you!

RELATIONSHIP COMMUNICATION

How to Resolve Any Conflict With Your Partner, Avoid Communication Mistakes, Create Deeper Intimacy, and Gain Healthy Conflict Resolution in Your Relationship

Emily Richards

© Copyright 2020 by Emily Richards. All right reserved.

The work contained herein has been produced with the intent to provide relevant knowledge and information on the topic on the topic described in the title for entertainment purposes only. While the author has gone to every extent to furnish up to date and true information, no claims can be made as to its accuracy or validity as the author has made no claims to be an expert on this topic. Notwithstanding, the reader is asked to do their own research and consult any subject matter experts they deem necessary to ensure the quality and accuracy of the material presented herein.

This statement is legally binding as deemed by the Committee of Publishers Association and the American Bar Association for the territory of the United States. Other jurisdictions may apply their own legal statutes. Any reproduction, transmission or copying of this material contained in this work without the express written consent of the copyright holder shall be deemed as a copyright violation as per the current legislation in force on the date of publishing and subsequent time thereafter. All additional works derived from this material may be claimed by the holder of this copyright.

The data, depictions, events, descriptions and all other information forthwith are considered to be true, fair and accurate unless the work is expressly described as a work of fiction. Regardless of the nature of this work, the Publisher is exempt from any responsibility of actions taken by the reader in conjunction with this work. The Publisher acknowledges that the reader acts of their own accord and releases the author and Publisher of any responsibility for the observance of tips, advice, counsel, strategies and techniques that may be offered in this volume.

INTRODUCTION

Thank you very much for purchasing *Relationship Communication*. I sincerely appreciate that you have done so. With this book, my mission is to help you and your partner form the deepest and most trusting bond that you can in your relationship endeavors. I wish to do this by giving you advice on relationship communication, as it is the glue that holds all stable relationships together. That is what we want. Stability is critical for the foundation of any relationship, lest it crumbles and falls apart before you have the chance to build it up. I hope beyond hope that my book helps accomplish and tackle, in part, some of the obstacles that you may come across in your relationship endeavors. Together, we can grow, learn, overcome obstacles, and resolve conflicts. I want this book to be a guiding light that will help you navigate those waters. I hope that I have accomplished that task sufficiently.

Throughout this book, we will cover, in a series of chapters and subchapters, many topics revolving around relationship communication. We will be going over what relationship communication is, what it means, and how it pertains to your life. I will also go over the different forms of communication that we can use, such as verbal, signed, written, body language, and communication through physical touch. Then, we will move on to conflict resolution and the steps involved to overcome it in the best possible way. We will go over ways to avoid conflict, methods of treading the waters of conflict calmly and constructively, and things to be avoided in a conflict.

After all of that is discussed, we will go into the most common relationship communication mistakes that people make, as well as how to resolve them. We will further that resolve by discussing empathy and its positive impact on our relationships and emotional health.

Then comes the steamy subject: Intimacy. Yes, believe it or not, communication plays a big and constructive role in heating things up in the bedroom. From passionate discussions to borders and expectations to making one another feel appreciated, communication is as intertwined as the two of you will be after reading the chapter.

To wrap it all up, we will recap on healthy conflict resolution, as it is a big subject in many budding *and* developed relationships, and then we will finish it off with a nice discussion about how to talk about difficult subjects in a trusting and comforting relationship environment as well as what the five languages of love are and how to identify and incorporate them into your relationships.

Though there are many relationship books on the market today, I am grateful that you have chosen this one. I made sure to fill it with the most enriching, honest, and helpful information on the subject matter that is available today. I hope that this book enlightens you and strengthens your relationship, and I wish you the best in the days to come. I sincerely believe that if you follow the advice in this book, your relationship will be much more open, strong, and fulfilling for both you and your partner. I hope you enjoy it!

CHAPTER 1
The Basics: What Is Relationship Communication?

To begin, let us answer the most basic question that is posed when one picks up this book: What is relationship communication? How we define this concept will shape our understanding of the chapters to come and solidify the hoops we must jump through to gain the most peaceful, intimate, durable, and loving bond that we can with our partner.

What Relationship Communication Means

Relationship communications, in the simplest terms, is exactly what it sounds like. It is the communication between individuals who are in a relationship, but what does that mean? Proper relationship communication is imperative to keeping a relationship healthy because it allows that relationship to be open, honest, and non-secretive.
There is no way in our common realm of understanding to read a person's mind. Therefore, to know your partner's needs and wants, or to communicate your own needs and wants to them, you must be able to relay that information. That is why healthy relationship communication is a must. Without it, anger, confusion, frustration, and distrust have a nasty habit of seeping into a relationship.
At its very core, you can say that relationship communication is all about proper connections and pathways for the open and honest transfer of basic needs, thoughts, feelings, wants, and ideas in a relationship. It is a deep conversation that goes past the daily small talk that we all engage in, and it reaches the root of feelings and views on life itself and daily obstacles. A good starting point in any relationship is to let your partner know that you care, that you are there to listen, and to both have an open dialogue about your personalities, short and long-term goals, morals, and more that will pertain to your lives and your relationship together.
It's also good to let your partner know that you are there for them and that you can quietly sit and listen to what they have to say engagingly. Let them know that you are their number one fan, support system, and confidant, and hopefully, they can do the same for you. Get into each other's heads through proper, deep dialogue and learn to understand each other's point of view so you can avoid conflict down the road. We will talk more about that later. For now, we will delve deeper into what it means to communicate and how relationship communication works.

How Does Relationship Communication Work?

Now that we know what relationship communication is, how does it work? Well, it means that you need to put in the effort to properly communicate your thoughts, needs, wants, etc. with your partner. This can be through body language, spoken words, written words and images, and physical acts. We will go over each of these communication outlets here to further your understanding of how each works and how you can apply them to your relationship moving forward.

Body Language

Many people don't notice body language concerning communication, but it is incredibly critical, whether obviously or subtly, to one's understanding of the message that their partner gives off or is trying to give off. Body language can be as small as folding one's hands together or as big as knitted eyebrows and an angry frown. It all coincides with communication.

Body language is one of the unspoken forms of communication that we often miss unless it's blatantly obvious, such as a frown, wink, or smile. It is a great indication of emotion, and it is a very intimate way to know someone by being able to read their body to tell how they are feeling. It will greatly strengthen your relationship and your communication capabilities once you and your partner learn how to read each other's bodies.

Once you can read the body language of your partner, and not confuse it as this can lead to relationship stumbles and obstacles, it will be incredibly beneficial for you both. It is also very intimate and can make you and your partner feel much closer when just a passing glance lets you know how they are feeling.

With that in mind, it is important to pay attention to your body language so that you do not give off the wrong impression from day to day. For example, when you are sitting with your partner, take care to avoid crossing your arms or legs, for that makes you seem distant, disinterested in their company or conversation or uncomfortable. If it is comfortable for you to sit this way, convey that to your partner, so they do not feel offended or get the wrong idea in a situation such as this.

Rolling your eyes is another negative form of body language and expression. It is snarky, disrespectful in most cases, and hurtful if you are not joking. If you are joking, make sure to voice that and make sure you can read positive body language in your partner. If your partner stiffens, frowns, or slumps their shoulders, it is an indication that you may need to apologize and clarify the situation. Always follow up an action or an ambiguous form of body language with a verbal affirmation of what you have done so that your partner does not get the wrong idea.

Try to be as open as you can with your body language, so the atmosphere is warmer and more inviting. This will keep away negative energies and emotions on a more subtle level, pushing away the possibility for further complications down the road.

Maintaining eye contact is also very important because whether you believe so or not, it shows that you are truly listening to what your partner is saying. If you speak or listen when looking away from your partner, you may seem distant or disinterested in the conversation, or your partner.

With all of that said, it is easy to see that body language is an important first step to recognizing the basics of communication in your relationship! Maintain positive body language throughout your relationship, so your partner always feels appreciated. It will be the detriment of the relationship if you are not consistent because if you start out strong and then let it all fade over time, the relationship will crumble. Something as simple as a smile can work wonders even if you don't realize it.

Examples of body language communication, direct or indirect, include:
- Crossed arms during a conversation or argument, symbolizing closing oneself off to the conversation and being angry, upset, or confrontational, or putting up proverbial walls
- A blush, meaning embarrassment, a flush of passion, nervousness, fear, or another strong but subsidiary emotion
- Tapping one's foot or fingers, symbolizing nervousness or impatience
- A smile, frown, knitted brows, or other facial cues
- Opening your arms out wide as an indication that you would like to embrace

Spoken Words

The act of speaking words, or using sign language for the hearing impaired, is the most common and easily identifiable form of communication that we know of today. It is direct, easily understood, and telling. Therefore, it is easy to utilize speech for dialogue between two romantic partners. However, it is also easy to wield as a weapon, so one must be careful with this form of communication as well.

Speaking our thoughts, feelings, ideas, and desires is critical for fostering a healthy relationship between two people. When you voice a problem, it can be resolved. When you tell your partner that you care about them, it is heartwarming and strengthens the relationship.

Words are powerful. Yes, actions speak louder than words, but the words are the stepping stone for further action. Use your words to the advantage of your relationship and strive to be open, honest, expressive, and affectionate. This is a wonderful way to get a good foundation started for your relationship.

When you have an argument, you speak. When you tell your partner "I love you" for the first time, you often speak those words. Words are so incredibly intertwined into any relationship that this is not an area that can be skipped over. Use your words very carefully, and think every sentence through before you speak it. You can apologize all you want, but you can never take back the words you say, no matter how hard you try. Always speak thoughtfully, caringly, and honestly.

I cannot stress this point enough because it is imperative going forward in this book and in the life of your relationship as a whole. Make sure you are intentional and careful with your words, and it will go a long way. Examples of spoken word communication include:
- A phone call
- Speaking directly, person to person
- A voicemail
- A song
- A question or query
- A compliment
- Words of affirmation
- Verbal criticism

Written Words and Images/Media Communication

In this day and age, this section might as well be called texting, but as I know that there is more to written words than that, I will leave the section titled as is. I want to hope and believe that couples still leave sweet written notes and messages for their partner. Therefore, I will put that as an example of the personal touch of communication in this section as well.

With that clarified, I will say that written word communication is just about on par with spoken these days. With the amount of texting and instant messaging that we do every day, it is nearly taking over our overall communication. With that said, you must take a lot of care when you communicate with your partner.

The good thing is that it is a lot easier to think about what you type or write before you send it. You can erase, backspace, and rewrite instead of blurting out words verbally that you cannot take back. That is an advantage. The disadvantage is that we often send messages very quickly without truly thinking them through or proofreading them. Try not to get into this habit.

Another concern with written communication is that emotions do not translate well through text, even with pictures or emojis. Make sure to write eloquently enough to get your point across while avoiding dialogue that could be construed as vague, harsh, blunt, or sarcastic. Make sure to back up your words with verbal communication, as well, when you have the change so that miscommunication and confusion do not occur. This is imperative if you want to maintain healthy communication in a relationship. People find their meanings and jump to conclusions when reading things quite often, so it is best to make sure that you accurately convey your message.

Examples of written word or image communication include:

- Emails
- Texts
- Emojis
- Instant messages
- Handwritten notes, such as a small note slipped into a lunch bag, a sticky note on the window, or a message on the mirror
- Magnets rearranged on the refrigerator
- A steamy note on the bathroom mirror made from the condensation
- A small picture indicating love or some other emotion
- A painting
- A greeting card
- A funny video

Physical Acts

Much like body language, physical acts are a great nonverbal way to communicate your feelings and intentions through touch. This is likely the most intimate of the forms of communication I will be covering in this chapter. It is more direct than body language as well, so it is easier to convey your intentions in this manner. However, try to follow up on your physical actions with verbal dialogue to make sure consent is agreed upon, and messages are conveyed correctly.

There are obvious and ambiguous forms of physical communication, and it is important to note that difference. Obvious forms of physical communication include crying, which is most often associated with either sadness or joy. It's easy to notice if someone is crying with sadness, as they will likely frown or slump their shoulders. If they are crying with joy, it is likely accompanied by bright eyes and a smile. You can always follow up on these actions with words for further clarity. If your partner is crying, make sure to ask if your partner is ok and offer comfort in either of the two situations I have mentioned here.

A more ambiguous form of physical communication, and one that needs a bit of verbal affirmation and consent, could be something along the lines of a kiss or the action of placing your hand on your partner's leg. You need to back these up with spoken communication in order to assess your partner's reaction and convey your intentions. For example, if you place your hand on your partner's leg, it could be an invitation for intimacy or a simple caress of comfort. Verbally express your intentions while asking if your partner is ok with the acts involved. This second layer of communication will help you both remain comfortable and will eliminate an awkward moment of confusion.

Make sure to curb your more aggressive physical communication, such as grabbing your partner forcefully by the arm, getting in their face during an argument, or pushing them away. This can lead to many negative outcomes down the road. Try to replace that aggression with thoughtful words and honest concerns that are spoken calmly.

On the flip side, try to express warm emotions and feelings more frequently, such as warm hugs, sweet kisses, hand holding, and more to let your partner know that you are there, you care, and you want to be near them. Even the little things show how much you appreciate your partner, such as when you brush the hair from your partner's face, lay your head on your partner's shoulder, or simply sit next to your partner when you watch a movie. Try not to distance yourself too much, and always let your partner know that you are there, with proper boundaries if necessary.

Examples of indirect or direct physical communication include:
- Crying as an open and direct communication of sadness, anger, or frustration
- Laying your head on your partner's shoulders and/or wrapping your arms around them to show you need their support, love, affection, touch, etc.
- Placing a hand on your partner's leg, indicating a want for physical touch for comfort or intimacy
- Kissing your partner on the cheek to show you care for them but aren't necessarily initiating sexual intimacy
- When you place a hand on your partner's shoulder to show that you are listening and that you are there. It is a connective gesture that can strengthen your relationship, similar to holding hands.

How Respect and Trust Tie into Healthy Relationship Communication

Almost as important, if not more important, than proper dialogue in a relationship is respect and trust. These tie into the stability of the relationship and hold it together like glue. Communication ties right into that steadfastness as your words and actions dictate your ability to trust, receive trust, respect, and receive respect. Your words and actions can either hold your relationship together or cause it to crumble and fall apart, just like trust and respect can.

Always, always back up your words with proper actions and stay consistent with what you say and do. If you tell your partner that you love them, back it up with words of affirmation, affection, physical touch if they are comfortable with that, fidelity, and respect for your partner and their things. If you say you will do something, do it. If you say you won't do something, don't do it. If you tell them something, back it up with an action that affirms your words. It's all in the consistency, which we will cover soon.

Respect is important, for if you do not respect each other you will never truly listen to or acknowledge what one another says. Furthermore, never belittle your partner with your words. Just as your words can lift up and support your partner in a cocoon of love, they can cut like a sharp knife and cut away the happiness and security of your relationship. Words are powerful, and they are critical for maintaining proper respect in a relationship. Make sure your partner always knows that you appreciate what they do, and follow up any positive action with words of affirmation! It will make your partner feel special, and it will foster the reciprocation of respect and positive reinforcement in the relationship.

Contempt and condescension are detrimental to a relationship, and these are the opposite of respect. Keep them at bay, and if your partner does not do something you like, instead of speaking down, lift them up with encouragement and constructive criticism. Meet your partner at their level, and never look down upon them. This is destructive and damaging, will lower your partner's self-esteem, and will make your partner feel unloved and unappreciated.

Just remember this: The closer you get to your partner, romantically, sexually, emotionally, or otherwise, the stronger your respect should be for that partner. Respect should not fade over time, for love will not grow that way. Love and respect should go hand in hand, so the deeper your relationship gets, the greater the level of respect should become. Weak levels of respect lead to a weakened relationship overall, and over time.

Now, do not confuse respect with a level of formality. You can let your guard down around your partner. Just don't be rude! Show them the same level of respect that you expect yourself. Treat your partner with kindness, care, and respect. You don't have to be rigid by any means, just practice common courtesy and let your partner know how much you appreciate what they do every day. This can be as simple as a smile, a hug, a compliment, or saying please and thank you. It does not have to be complicated or difficult by any means. Just don't harm your relationship by shutting off your connection to your partner with harsh words and disrespect. Remember, relationships should flow well and remain open and honest, but not harsh. Minimize the friction and simply be kind and courteous to the one you care for.

Trust is critical for letting your partner know that you believe what they say and that you can both make faithful promises to one another. Trust can be as simple as giving your partner the benefit of the doubt before you jump to conclusions, or it can be as intricate as believing that when they go out with friends, they will always come home to you, and you know that they have been true. You should know that you can always trust and fall back onto your partner, knowing that they will catch you and hold you up. The strength of your bond is built on a foundation of trust and honesty, and you must cherish that in order to keep that strength steadfast.

Trust builds comfort. It builds a cushion with which to fall back on when you are weary or struggling. Fill that cushion, your relationship, with the padding of accountability and dependability so neither you nor your partner will ever crash-land into rocky terrain. Hold each other up, develop a support system for each other, and stay true, always, to your words and actions. There is nothing more beneficial in a relationship than a strong foundation of trust and support. If you know you can always rely on each other, there is nothing that can bring you down.

Another way to build trust is to try new things, accomplish tasks together to build dependability, and take small risks or leaps of faith to see if you come out stronger together. Putting in an effort toward a reward together will make you both come out more fulfilled and with a tighter bond. Go on a romantic adventure together, somewhere neither of you has ever been before, and traverse its waters, overcome its obstacles, and have fun! Let your walls come down, if even for a brief period, and let loose! See if your partner can hold you up as you soar to new heights, and learn how to depend on one another with no bars held. It can be very enlightening, thrilling, and beneficial to you both as people and as a unit. Step outside your comfort zone with your partner, and maybe they will follow suit and do the same. Stretch and grow and support one another through those growing pains so you can develop both independently and together as one. This will help your relationship reach new heights, and it will feel good, too!

It is also best to maintain the ability to be trusted and respected, as well as the ability to stay sincere and stable. Always be honest, stay true to your word, keep your promises, and back up every statement with a positively reinforced action that affirms your dialogue. Stay faithful and do not waver. Keep your promises true, and do not break them without proper cause or without discussing it first with your partner. Stay open, be honest, and let your partner know ahead of time if anything is going to be changed.

A relationship is a rock that must not be moved, only grown upon and developed. It has to be stable, unshakeable, and true. If either of the individuals in a relationship shatters or move it with unfaithfulness or lies, it can wreak havoc on that relationship. The rock will crumble and fall with dishonesty and blatant disrespect of your partner. Keep this in mind going forward, and remember it before starting any new relationship or rekindling an old one.

Another good point to take note of is to be open and vulnerable. Once you are comfortable in your relationship, it's ok to let your walls down a bit so you can breathe and communicate openly. If you have been hurt in the past and are wary about opening up, a good starting point is letting your partner know that so that you don't convey a distance or a barrier that cannot be shaken.

Let your partner take you in and comfort you, and build trust together so that you can start the process of breaking down those walls. This is where true trust comes in. It may be difficult starting out, but if you maintain proper communication and faith in one another everything will turn out fine. As long as you are both open and honest, those walls will come down naturally and comfortably, I'm sure.

Consistency and Its Important Role in Relationship Communication

As I've mentioned, one of the most important things to remember about your communication in your relationship is consistency. Consistency eliminates confusion, makes it harder to slip up and do something that will negatively impact your relationship, and allows for a common, stable ground with which your relationship can stand on.

Consistency, as it pertains to a relationship and the communication therein, can be best defined as being a cocktail of repetitive, positive behaviors that remain predictable over time. Examples of these behaviors include trust, dependability, strong desire, the need to maintain the bond with your partner, companionship, predictability, solid communication practices, and the absence of false personality or pretending to feel something that you do not.

The last point in that paragraph, regarding false feelings, is a big point that hits home regarding trust. Do not live a lie and pretend to feel a certain way when you do not honestly feel that way. It paves a foundation of dishonesty and will shatter easily over time, leading to the downfall of a relationship. It is very hard to consistently hold a lie, so try to avoid it at all costs.

Consistency also pertains to how you treat your partner. Stay consistent in how you treat your partner so that you do not catch your partner off guard or unintentionally hurt that individual. If you greet your partner a certain way every day, do not change it suddenly, or it could harm your partner's perception of the situation and cause your partner to think that your relationship has changed course without their knowledge. The communication of thoughts, intentions, and information in general within your relationship must remain consistent to avoid confusion in the short and long-term.

Consistency thoroughly ties into the previous idea of trust and dependability in a relationship. If consistency is kept, you can be relied upon more easily, and you will also have more predictable dialogue, so your partner does not have to be fearful of your reaction in certain situations. It also makes you more dependable, and it helps further reinforce the stability of your relationship.

Consistency will also make you and your partner feel more relaxed. You won't have to be on edge or walk on eggshells around your partner, because that foundation of consistency will be there. Just stay true to your character and your relationship, and don't waver regarding how you react and respond. In the end, if you heed these words, your relationship will be a hard egg to crack.

CHAPTER 2
How To Resolve Any Conflict With Your Partner

This step may seem like a bit of a tricky one, or even too good to be true, but it's not, and I will show you why. Taking the proper steps to build a good foundation for your communication in your relationship, and following the guidelines I am about to show you, will pave the way for smooth sailing in the long run. No matter what relationship storms brew, or what tries to strike the two of you down, you can weather the storm and smooth those waters with ease. The key is communication, conflict resolution, and respect.

To start, I will say that arguments, when they do not get out of hand, can actually be healthy for a relationship, contrary to popular belief. There is no perfect relationship, and if you have a relationship with no conflict, and no give and take, then there is something amiss. Either one or both are pushing down their feelings and not acknowledging issues, which is very dangerous, or they have both shut off completely and would rather ignore or avoid issues. Neither of these things is good, and it is the opposite of healthy relationship communication.

The blossoming of arguments in a relationship is actually a sign of relationship growth. It shows that both of you are comfortable enough in the relationship to let your walls down a bit and share your differences and discomforts. It is just one of the many forms of relationship communication. The catch is that it will either foster growth in your relationship or tear it down, depending on how it is handled.

Everyone is different in some way, so the views of one versus another may not jive too well in the beginning. You have to sort through that and compromise, and it all has to be out in the open in a healthy way so that you may resolve your differences positively.

If you have an issue, your partner and you have to discuss that issue, or it will never be resolved. It will just build and build and build until the lid bursts off, and it becomes an absolute, big, chaotic mess full of hurt and confusion. You have to communicate. By resolving these disagreements, in a way that is healthy and non-aggressive, it can create a deeper bond of understanding between you and your partner and bring you closer as a couple. It also breeds stability and trust, and a wonderful sense of comfort if you both know that not every disagreement will end in a sparring match.

Now, if a disagreement occurs, let's go over some various steps and guidelines for what to, and not to, do.

Consider Each Other's Perspectives

When in an argument, make sure not to jump to conclusions prematurely. Before you speak, take a moment to consider where your partner is coming from and why. Take a moment, stop, reflect, breathe, think, and then speak. Do not attack, mind you, and do not speak from assumption. Phrase any assumptions as a question to assess your partner's point of view. Specifically, ask what is troubling your partner and why, and with the foundation of trust you have built, you can accept and believe their answer. Then build upon that answer, state your side, and calmly discuss the perspectives each of you has so you can find the root of the issue.

This is one of the most critical parts of any argument. In order to avert the attention away from the individuals and the raw emotions, you can focus on the matter at hand and attack *that* together so you can fall back onto common and stable ground. You can even dance a little jig once it is all said and done if that's something you like to do.

Basically, what I'm saying here is that you should always use empathy, trust, and intuition to assess the situation and view the world from your partner's eyes. This is not to say that you should assume what they feel right off the bat, but you can get a better picture of how they feel if you let your walls down and step into their shoes a bit. It will build trust, as well, if they know that you consider their opinion enough to take the time to feel out the situation. You will bond over it, and the issue may just resolve all on its own if you get to the root of understanding where your partner is coming from.

Do Not Yell!

Yelling, instead of speaking in a calm tone, can make it much harder for points to get across, as the aggression will ultimately spark fear, aggression, pain, or other negative responses in the recipient of the shouting. It will just meddle the auditory reception of the words and throw a veil of disinterest over what you are saying if you start out in a screaming match. Yelling is never a good idea.

All yelling will do is get you both so fired up that you will never resolve the issue. When you feel like you are about to yell or fly off the handle, calmly excuse yourself, let your partner know that you both need to cool off, and go take some deep breaths and reflect before coming back. The key here is that you should not go back to the conversation, until you are sure that you are both calmed down.

However, do not leave the argument completely and ignore it without revisiting it. Revisit the argument that same day, after you have both calmed down, and speak calmly. Talk through each of the issues separately, try not to get off-topic or too chaotic, and make sure each of the issues is resolved before moving on to the next.

Speaking in a calm but clear voice is going to take you both so much farther than starting out a conversation with raised, high-pitched voices. It's much harder to grasp the concepts of the discussion if volumes and pitches are rising sky-high and fluctuating. The human ear picks up on these fluctuations and focuses on them, which could cause a spike in anxiety and the fight or flight response in your adrenal glands. This pitches you into a more primal mindset that can toss you into attack mode and throw the conversation way off base. So, breathe, lower your voice, and speak. Communicate with your words and not your volume and harsh tone. This is true communication, and it will ultimately resolve the problem much faster.

Do Not Belittle Your Partner

Belittling your partner can hurt their self-esteem and cause negative friction between the both of you, opening the door for disrespect and harmful words that neither of you means but can never take back. Tread carefully here. You and your partner are supposed to be equals in your relationship. Do not let one of you dominate over the other and force submission in any situation. This can be damaging to your relationship and the self-esteem of the parties involved. Don't insight a power-struggle. Cultivate a conversation that can lead to resolution and peace.

Next, both of you should focus on self-esteem. It is an important and critical factor in any conflict resolution. It is essential to standing your ground in an argument and not wavering in your decisions, as well as maintaining good communication without getting anxious. Bolstering your self-esteem, without getting haughty, can actually build a good foundation for avoiding future disagreements.

Finally, avoid being passive-aggressive, and strive to be direct but not condescending. Passive aggression can make your partner feel belittled just because you are petty enough not to tackle the issue head-on, resorting to derogatory means that are subtle and confusing.

To recap a bit, these are the possible negative outcomes of low self-esteem that can come from belittling your partner:

- Heightened sensitivity upon taking things too personally over time, as it can lead to feelings of being attacked or looked down upon in most situations
- The raising of walls that we discussed should be comfortably taken down with trust.
- The need to be very defensive in otherwise non confrontational situations
- Snap decisions, impulse, and high reaction rates
- A fear of speaking true needs wants, and feelings in situations where they are required
- An overactive need to people-please
- High levels of harmful anxiety or even depression
- An inability to take responsibility for actions, personal needs, and feelings which can lead to self-neglect and poor health

- Dishonesty, either to oneself or one's partner
- High expectations of oneself or others, inflating the inability to reach one's goal of supposed perfection

Find the Root of the Issue, and Separate the Person from the Problem

Many arguments seem one way on the surface but stem from a deeper-rooted issue below the surface. Have an open and honest dialogue with your partner and lay it all on the table so the two of you can sort through the issues and find the root of the cause. Furthermore, make sure to target the issue and not the person involved in the argument. The issue is the problem, not the person posing this issue. Do not attack your partner, but discuss the problem head-on to avoid any ambiguity or negative emotions. It is not, for instance, the person that you are truly frustrated with. It is the situation, so change it for your good and for the betterment of your partner. Your relationship will thank you, I'm sure.

The root of the matter is normally insecurity, an unsolved emotional issue, or something that one or the other person has been putting off for a while that is finally bubbling to the surface. Whatever the reason, try to make it your priority to pinpoint this main root so you can dig it up and hopefully resolve it first so the outlying issues will fall away with it. The smaller surface issues normally stem from the root cause of the problem as a whole.

For instance, if you are arguing with your partner about a fear that you have, let those walls down and confide in your partner. Let them know what scares you. It is not your partner that scares you, but it is the fear that you have projected upon that person. See how I separated that? Now, you can resolve it with honest dialogue.

Next, try to approach the issue as a team, not as two separate entities fighting. Fight the problem, not the person, and work as a team, together, to resolve it for the betterment of your relationship as a whole. Fight those fears off with encouragement, trust, and love and fall into each other's arms once it is resolved and tell each other how much you appreciate one another for having the strength to come forward and tackle such a difficult subject together.

To Resolve, and Not to Attack

The intent of a healthy conflict resolution, and the approach thereof, is to calmly talk out the problem and find a compromise. Resolve the conflict and move on. The purpose of a disagreement is not to attack one another or point out who is wrong. It is to calmly explain each of your sides, find the root cause of the disagreement, and talk it all out.

Arguments are not supposed to be a tug-of-war. It is not about who wins or loses, but it is about the ability to resolve the issue proposed between the two of you. If you do win an argument, so to speak, there will still be residual resentment that will hurt the relationship and your partner, and it will lower your partner's self-esteem, which is not the goal that you want to achieve.

If all else fails, give your partner the benefit of the doubt and agree to disagree. If it is something that does not affect your health, your life, or your relationship, it is ok to just let it go, agree to disagree, and forget about it. This is for small matters that will not matter in the long run of your relationship. This is not a fix for big issues that directly affect one or both of you, but it is ok to just let some small things slide off your back and agree to disagree. It will minimize the need for further conflicts and it will diffuse the situation.

Above All Else, Do Not Hold a Grudge

The detriment of relationships is holding a grudge. Getting negative feelings and pushing them down and away, only to have them pop up aggressively at inopportune moments is very damaging to a relationship. Always try to resolve an issue before this happens, and learn to forgive and trust your partner. Forgiveness is not only for the other person, but it is also beneficial to your wellbeing, peace of mind, and happiness. Forgiveness, when warranted, is a very healthy attribute of a good relationship that has a solid flow of communication.

Try not to stockpile your resentments over time. If something is bothering you, say it. If there is a conflict, resolve it. If the issue has been resolved, forgive it and let it slide off your back and into oblivion, but you must work things out as they come up, or they could turn into grudges and resentment. Communicate what is bothering you or your partner will not know what they did wrong to harbor that resentment, and it can make your partner resent you back. This is not healthy, so try to avoid it at all costs.

Forgiveness goes hand in hand with trust and respect. If you truly care for your partner, and your own wellbeing, learn to forgive them when they have done wrong, especially if they have apologized. Once the issue has been resolved, it is finished, and there is no need to bring it up again or use it as ammunition against your partner. This is petty, damaging, and wrong. It will not lead to a healthy relationship or communication therein.

CHAPTER 3
Avoid Common Mistakes

Mistakes will undoubtedly be made in any relationship. It's common, it's natural, and it's likely unavoidable. However, how we tackle those mistakes and react to them can make or break a relationship before it has the chance to blossom. Relationship communication mistakes can at times become sneaky and pop up when you least expect it, such as when you start finally getting comfortable enough with your partner to show your true colors. Communication is key here, and we will go over some of the most common mistakes that we must avoid and remedy with proper communication practices. Don't let a pattern of unhealthy communication practices form before you have the opportunity to identify and stem them. This chapter will help you get on the right track! Let's get started!

Jumping to Conclusions/Assumptions

Rash decisions almost always have negative outcomes. Instead of prematurely assuming things about your partner without proper evidence, simply ask your partner so that your partner can clear the air, and no feelings are hurt. Be honest and come forth with any issues so that your partner can either confirm or deny them before an argument ensues. Assumptions can severely damage a relationship, so try to curb them before they break out and strike at your relationship.

This is a paraphrase from an ancient proverb, but it is very wise. The proverb says that it is not smart to answer a question that you yourself pose before hearing the correct answer from the person whom you are questioning. In order to get to the root of any situation, you must have adequate information and view the problem from all possible perspectives so that you get the context correct. Many things, when viewed out of context, can be severely misconstrued. When push comes to shove, listen with your ears, and do not assume with your eyes or your mind.

Oftentimes, we project our hang-ups from past relationships and past occurrences onto our current relationships. This is damaging for many reasons, but it will primarily damage your partner's trust of you and your ability to comfortably navigate the relationship without walking on eggshells. If your partner believes that you will always jump to conclusions, it can cause that person to pull back and withhold affection, emotions, thoughts, and intimacy from you. Your partner will try to tiptoe around situations, which will likely cause your assumptions to flare even more. Eliminate this realm of possibility by simply being open and honest with your partner and believing that they will do the same for you.

When you have an inkling about something before you do anything stop and breathe. Do not open your mouth or take any action until you give yourself ample time to process the information and assess the potential outcomes. Never accuse, and always ask. This will eliminate the feeling your partner could have upon being attacked without probable cause. Think about it this way: Would you want your partner to jump to conclusions before you have been given the opportunity to defend yourself or explain the situation?

If the answer is no, then do not do that to your partner. Even if your answer is yes, don't do it to your partner. Treat your partner with the respect that you would want to be given in that type of situation. Pause, give your partner the benefit of the doubt, allow your partner to have the room to speak and allow yourself to be open enough to dig deeper into the situation to find the truth behind where your assumptions lead you. This will help you cultivate a safer, more trusting, and healthy relationship that you and your partner can find comfort and not conflict in. Suspend your judgment and allow solid evidence and fulfilling conversations to take hold, and you will do just fine.

Speaking on Impulse

Always think things through, and try not to blurt things out as soon as they pop into your head. Don't be one who word-vomits then picks up the pieces later. Try to hold your tongue and find the best routes for communication before you speak. This will save you a lot of headaches and conflicts down the road. Just because something comes to you, you have a piece that you think needs to be spoken, or you assume something, don't blurt it out without really thinking it through.

This also has a lot to do with timing. Bringing up issues, or starting an argument, at the wrong time or place can put a strain on your relationship. It is poor room-reading and communication to act on impulse and bring things up out of the blue or during inopportune times of the day.

Impulsivity can cause confusion and hurt, especially if it comes out of the blue and surprises your partner, who unfortunately cannot read your mind. Impulsivity can also trigger you to say things you may not mean or that may need to stay in your head to protect your partner from getting hurt, regardless of if that impulsive thought is true or not. In the end, it will only push your partner away and cause your partner to view you with potential anxiety as they are not sure what you will say next or when.

Don't allow your relationship to spiral out of control just because you cannot control your thoughts and your speech. Sometimes, too much communication and bluntness can be damaging. It's all about a balance and getting a good sense of your partner's sensitivities. Something can sound really good in your head but actually appear very hurtful from your partner's perspective.

Raising Your Voice

This was touched on in the previous chapter but is important to note again because it is a common error that many make during the course of a relationship. Try not to have a short fuse and resort to yelling just to have your voice heard during angered or passionate moments where you converse. Having a loud voice actually does the opposite, as it creates tension and makes it harder to understand where you are coming from. Raised voices lead people to believe that you are speaking out of an irrational mindset and that your words stem from raw emotion and not calculated intellect.

Sacrificing Your Own Happiness

Sacrificing your own happiness will wreak havoc on your emotional stability, mental health, and overall view of the world. It is not healthy for you, your partner, or your relationship and must be remedied in order to build a stable romantic foundation. Let's go over some of the ways we sacrifice our happiness and what we can do to change those actions for the better.

Apologizing After Every Debacle

Apologizing, though you don't have to, after every situation where you assume you are in the wrong, is an unhealthy practice. It does not allow your partner to admit their wrongdoings, and it can severely damage the overall trust and stability of your relationship. It will create issues with your boundaries, cause an unhealthy pattern of negative consistency, and give your partner free rein to do whatever they want, as you will simply apologize for them. This is not fair to you or the relationship.

Apologizing too much also hurts your self-esteem. It causes confusion as you start questioning every action you make and feeling that you are not good enough to do anything right. It is a big factor in relationship anxiety and can mar the communication flow in a relationship. It can also cause a gut or impulse reaction where you start apologizing for every mistake in your relationship and your life. Tell yourself this: If you are apologizing for every aspect of your relationship, is the relationship worth sustaining? Why keep something that you always have to feel sorry for? Change your ways quickly, or you may slip into the mindset that you should get out lest your apologies overrule your life.

The best thing to do is, to be honest, and communicate openly with your partner. See things from both perspectives, and yes, apologize for what you do wrong, but do not excuse the wrongdoings of your partner. Furthermore, never apologize out of fear or to simply get your partner off your back. That is incredibly damaging, and it also enables negative behavior that will send you both spiraling out of control. There is no stability in this practice, so you will never find common ground or feel secure and safe in your relationship.

This simply communicates to your partner that they can do no wrong and that they can walk all over you with no consequence. Hold your partner accountable for your actions, and do not allow yourself to become a doormat. Do not allow dishonesty and deceit to seep into your relationship.

A great way to start combating this is to focus on your own inner strength and insecurities. By mending your own potentially broken spirit and self-consciousness, you can grow stronger in your relationship and stand on even ground.

Being too Submissive

Don't roll over and expose your belly like a lamb for the slaughter, or it will damage your emotional, mental, and potentially physical wellbeing. Set up clear and concise boundaries at the start of the relationship and be consistent about it. Be caring, but firm, and reaffirm those boundaries without wavering so that there are stable ground and common understanding throughout your relationship. This will ultimately eliminate confusion in the long run.

Bending so far until you ultimately break and damage yourself is not a sign of undying love for your partner, it is a sign that you are harming your own wellbeing and the wellbeing of the relationship dynamic. In some ways, it is just as disrespectful to your partner as it is to yourself. You are not allowing your partner the room to grow as a person and contribute as much as they need to in the relationship.

Don't let your partner walk all over you. Set up boundaries, and stick to them so that you can strengthen yourself, strengthen your relationship, and keep yourself from being harmed.

Being too Dependent On/Being a Crutch

It is nice to feel like you are needed, but there is a limit. If your partner becomes too dependent on you, it can become a burden for you and a handicap for your partner. It is actually detrimental to their wellbeing as a person to become too codependent because it makes it harder for them to stand on their own if the time ever came for that to happen. No matter how much you care for a person, you have to be practical and realistic and set up boundaries to preserve your own independence.

Set realistic goals and expectations for both you and your partner so that you can reach them as a team while strengthening and supporting the person who is being too dependent. Once that person reaches a sufficient level of strength, branch your goals just enough so that the dependent person can grow to meet their own needs and gain independence and self-confidence. It does not have to happen all at once, but it must be consistent, and there must be progress for you both to be able to grow and for the relationship to survive.

If you take a tree, the relationship in this metaphor, and overburden one side while leaving the other side lacking in growth, the tree will bend over and eventually snap. Don't let the burdens your partner tosses at you bend the tree of your relationship. Share the burdens, overcome them together, and work on a team so that your relationship can grow to new heights and remain strong and firm.

Furthermore, resist the urge to fix every issue that comes up. Allow your partner to learn how to fix their own problems and pick themselves up after a fall. If you catch your partner every time they mess up or fail, they will learn that you will clean up their messes. If you let them self-correct, it will place less burden on you and allow your partner to grow as a person and become an equal, strengthening partner in the relationship.

The bottom line: Be each other's support systems while working as an equal team.

Being Too Distant

Being too distant can be just as bad as being an emotional crutch. It's just the other side of the negative communication spectrum. If you are too silent, ignore issues, use passive aggression, suppress your emotions, give off an aura of resentment, and hold grudges, it can spell the downfall of your relationship and lead to deep-rooted hurt and chaos in a relationship. All of those suppressed emotions are going to bubble to the surface eventually, and when it ruptures, it will greatly damage the entire relationship and the parties involved. Why don't we go over how to fix some of these issues before they begin?

The Silent Treatment

The silent treatment is, basically, the same as holding up a sign that says: "Back off! I don't want to let you in." This is bad. This makes your partner feel unappreciated and blocks off any attempts for your partner to try to remedy the situation for fear of making you more upset. It stops all possibilities of making things any better than they currently are. Negative emotions will continue to stew and get worse, neither of you will feel any relief, and the issue will never be resolved.

In any relationship, it is always best to have your issues out in the open, without aggression, and to be open enough and trusting enough to allow your partner in so that they can help fix the situation. It is unfair to be blatantly mad at someone without taking any action to make it better.

The silent treatment is just another way of phrasing passive-aggression. Sneering from the sidelines, making pointed snide comments, glaring from across the room, and blatantly removing yourself from the vicinity of your partner are examples of this. It is hurtful, it is unkind, and it will not make either of you feel better. Set your aggression aside and talk out your feelings. You will find that if you do this, you will easily makeup and embrace each other, and each other's differences, much easier.

Pushing Down Your Emotions

Pushing your emotions down and never touching them or acknowledging that they are there will break you from the inside out. It is like putting a lid on a pressure cooker and letting the steam accumulate until the entire cooker cracks open, and the contents spill out in the worst possible way. It is best to get your emotions out in the open in a way that you can control before they have the opportunity to lash out and cause unnecessary pain.

Commanding Actions

Commanding your partner is a way of belittling and looking down upon that person. It is destructive and it can lower the self-esteem of you both. If you are too abrasive and commanding in your communicative abilities, neither of you will truly feel at peace, nor will you be able to trust one another. It is about balance and a bit of give-and-take. Your relationship should be fluid and ever-changing for the positive. It should not be abrupt and full of orders and superfluous rules. It should be freeing, warm, comfortable, and stable. These next sections will go over some of the dos and don'ts you may want to take into account if you are in a position where you feel like you must command your partner.

Ultimatums

Ultimatums are a defense mechanism that can harm your situation far more than it will help. Yes, they are direct, but it backs your partner into a wall that is hard to get out of. It leads to rash decisions, hurt, and betrayal. They will make your partner feel trapped, and it will put unnecessary pressure on your relationship. They are ingenuine and push away the root of the problem that has caused you to make such a rash decision. It is best to avoid them at all costs.
Instead of giving two choices that are unshakeable, compromise. Negotiate and discuss your issues in a way that gives your partner wiggle room to improve and make conscious decisions. Don't make up their mind for them. Chances are if you give only two choices, your partner will choose the one you don't really want. Don't get dominant and aggressive if you truly care about your partner. Make a way for you both to be happy without jeopardizing your entire relationship because you feel entitled to it.

Nagging

Try not to harp on the little things, and once an issue has been discussed, don't bring it up over and over again. Let your partner self-correct, negotiate, and take time to process what needs to be done. This can lead to a massive amount of annoyance and frustration. Nobody likes to feel like their partner is their mom, following behind them at every turn with a broomstick and shouting commands.

Furthermore, don't bring up events from your partner's past that are long over and resolved. This can cause tension and stem your partner's trust for you, as your partner may think that you will simply judge them or jump to conclusions.

Negotiate and Compromise

Again, compromise is key here. Before resulting in a command and conquer tactic that will lead to a negative dominant-submissive dynamic instead of a team effort, try to speak openly with your partner and become willing to hear their point of view. Put each of your opinions out in the open so you can see both perspectives and find common ground. This will eliminate the frustration and confusion of over-pleasing each other at the cost of your own happiness.

Manipulation Leads to Destruction

We have gone over being over-dominant and over-submissive in a relationship, but within that realm of understanding, I will go over some of the reasons that manipulation in any of the forms discussed can be harmful. Examples of what manipulation lead to include:
- Self-esteem issues
- Codependency
- Resentment
- Lashing out
- Arguments
- A lack of trust
- Instability
- And more harmful outcomes

Thinking Your Partner Can Read Your Mind

When you have a thought, pet peeve, pesky emotional issue, or anything that you want or need your partner to know but are afraid to ask, don't bite your tongue or let it sit and stew. Your partner cannot read your mind, and it is unfair of you to assume so or to get angry if they act in a way that is not consistent with your mindset. You must vocalize your issues, hang-ups, and emotions in order for you and your partner to bring them out into the open and resolve them as a team.

Understanding comes from proper communication. Tell your partner how you are feeling and be as open and honest as you can be. Try not to fear how they will act or feel because if they are truly invested in the relationship, they will listen regardless and try to find a compromise that is best for the both of you. Be truly honest, for honesty plays a big, big part here. If you are not honest, and your partner trusts you, they will not think to assume the real answer when you give them a false answer. This can lead to confusion, miscommunication, heartbreak, hypocrisy, and massive arguments and resentments down the road. There is no way to be a team and remain on the same page if you are not completely honest. Even small lies add up and poke holes in a relationship. Tread these waters carefully.

Do not assume that your partner knows you well enough to pick up on things, even if you give off body signals or otherwise. Reinforce your body signals with words. Cut out any possibility of ambiguity or jumping to conclusions. It will save you a lot of headaches in the long run, and it will help your partner trust you more.

Ask for what you need in the relationship and lay it all out on the table, lest you hit a massive roadblock in your relationship that will simply drive a wedge that could have been resolved easily in the beginning. Communicating in a healthy manner will eliminate the root causes of misunderstandings and future arguments, and it will be beneficial for you both if there are no guessing games, assumptions, and conclusion jumping. Just use your communication skills and talk it out!

A Lack of Listening

An inability to listen, or simply choosing not to listen, is as bad as choosing not to speak up. It is a blatant form of disrespect for your partner, and it shows that you would rather ignore that person than hear their thoughts. Conflicts will never get resolved this way, and it can mean the detriment of your relationship in the long run. Be open enough to allow your partner to view you as a confidant so you can build upon your relationship and grow into a comforting solace of understanding, forgiveness, and dialogue.

A Lack of Forgiveness and Acceptance

Look, everyone has their issues and things they need to work on. Every bit of progress made toward a better goal should be encouraged and built upon. Accept each other's differences, forgive when forgiveness is due, and learn to accept little things that you may not like but are ingrained in the person you chose to be with. You cannot change or fix a person.

Accept the things you cannot change and work together as a team to fix the things that can be changed. Use the tools learned thus far to talk through your issues together so that you can come to a better understanding as a couple and learn how to trust and forgive one another.

CHAPTER 4
How To Embrace Empathy

Empathy may seem like it is simply soft and sweet on the surface, all sugar plums and hugs and fairies, but it is a very powerful component of a healthy relationship. It is not all about sensitivity and butterflies but is a sensitive and gentle relationship attribute that is very important. It is a strong, constructive force of understanding, and it will help you *relate* to your partner, which is a key aspect here, and part of the nomenclature of a relationship. It is the relations between two individuals that create a relationship, after all. Therefore, being able to relate to your partner in a *relation*ship is a central component to note. Empathy is present at the very core of a true relationship.

What is Empathy?

Since we're going to be covering empathy in this entire chapter, it is a good idea to clarify what empathy is, by definition, and how it applies to your relationship. Empathy is one's ability to connect with their partner's emotions and share those feelings with one another. It is also a compassionate, instinctive, and thoughtful ability to understand another person's feelings. It means to feel things alongside somebody else in order to gain a better understanding of those feelings and navigate them together compassionately. In this way, you can put yourself into the shoes of another and think as if those emotions are yours so you can gain the best consideration of them.

Empathy applies to a relationship in many ways. Empathy, within the scope of a relationship, boils down to how much you care about the wellbeing of your partner and their emotions to the same extent that you care about your own wellbeing and emotions. It's bringing your partner's emotions close and down to the level of your own. Proper empathy can make a huge difference in the health of your relationship.

There are actually three core forms of empathy, which I will go over next.

Cognitive Empathy

Cognitive empathy is the conscious decision to view things from the perspective of another individual. It is what people refer to when they use the phrase "putting yourself into someone else's shoes." It is not the general definition of empathy on its own, but a branch of empathy itself that is very useful in a relationship for the benefit of both parties involved. It is a good technique for negotiations and compromises so you and your partner can find common ground.

Because this form of empathy is more conscious, it is easy to avoid getting wrapped up in the emotions of the situation, which is good in some cases. You don't have to engage the emotions, only understand them and view the perspective of another individual to gain insight. This is, arguably, the least emotive form of empathy. It is more practical, rational, and logical. It has to do with empathetic thought and not emotion.

Emotional Empathy

This form of empathy, as its name suggests, is incredibly emotive. This is an endearing form of empathy that is wonderful to possess, but this is the one you need to be careful not to get too incredibly wrapped up in. With this form of empathy, you more directly feel the emotions of another person.

Think of a time where you have been watching a movie, and you cried during a sad part though you were in no way a part of the situation in the movie. This is a prime example of emotional empathy. Another example is feeling drawn to go adopt a new pet from the shelter after seeing a video of sad, abandoned animals. It is very easy to be swayed with this form of empathy, and while it is very sweet to be that way, tread carefully and keep it at a moderately high but healthy level.

It is good in that it helps us understand and connect with the feelings of our partners so that we know how to help them. It is a good skill for caretakers, mothers, healthcare workers, teachers, and those in a romantic relationship. It is a good tool to have when we need to respond to those in distress. Just try not to become a pushover or become manipulated by those who know you have a high level of compassion.

This form of empathy is what most think of when they hear the word empathy. It is deeply emotional, very kind, and very strong. It has often been referred to as emotional contagion, as you basically catch the emotions of others as if catching a cold from them. Just take your proverbial medicine, self-control, and you should be fine. Just don't go the complete opposite and become stoic and hardened.

Compassionate Empathy

Compassionate empathy is another form of empathy that most think of when they hear the word empathy if they do not immediately think of the emotional empathy that we possess. In fact, emotional and compassionate empathy normally go hand in hand, but they have their differences.

Compassionate empathy is a lot like sympathy, but deeper. While sympathy is feeling emotions that are similar to your own, compassionate empathy is taking the feelings of others and understanding them while feeling concern or, well, compassion for those people. Compassionate empathy is also different from sympathy in that an individual with compassionate empathy is more likely to act upon those feelings and aid or lessen the problems posed by the affected people and their emotions.

Compassionate empathy is less volatile and manipulatable than emotional empathy because the focus is not on your emotional tie to another individual, but the drive to help that individual. It is the most appropriate type of empathy for matters that are more vulnerable. It is a good middle ground between cognitive and emotional empathy. You won't become a basket case of emotions upon feeling what others feel, as with emotional empathy, and you won't be overly calculative with your understanding like cognitive empathy. You will calculate the situation, assess the feelings, but act upon them in a compassionate way that points the focus on the one you are helping without too intimately tying your emotions to theirs. You can be understanding and caring and give the best amount of help that you can in this situation.

The Balance of the Three Empathies

Think of it like this. Emotional empathy is very emotional and affects you, cognitive empathy is less emotional and specifically targets the problem, and compassionate empathy creates a good balance by being right in the middle of the two, feeling emotive enough to want to help while focusing on the issue *and* the person involved. Make sure to properly balance these to remain stable in your use of empathy and learn to identify which form is best for certain situations. Apply reason, remain in control, open your heart, and use it to the betterment of yourself and your relationship.

Empathy and Trust

Empathy is a big factor in the foundation of trust in a relationship, and it will deepen the intimacy and the feeling of connectivity in your relationship. You will feel more bonded, in a healthy way, and gain a sense of belonging with your partner. Empathy also makes it easier to notice when a problem occurs before it becomes a large issue because once you notice your partner's telling signals, which we will go into further in a moment, you can ask your partner openly about your perception of the signals they are giving off.

Their honesty, and your compassion, will help you both form a concrete solution to the potential issues hiding just below the surface of your partner's emotions. Being closely bonded and open enough in your relationship will help you utilize your empathy to reach below the surface and surmise how to help your partner.

Something that goes hand in hand with trust is forgiveness. When you become more empathetic and caring to your partner, your partner will feel listened to and appreciated. It will also make it easier to forgive one another once you gain the ability, through empathy, to catch a quicker and easier glimpse into your partner's point of view. You will be able to quickly react and avoid turning a blind eye to the negative emotions of your partner if the foundation of trust is there and forgiveness allows your heart to not cloud your eyes to these situations. It will ultimately strengthen your bond and bring you closer together.

The trust built with empathy can also help you foster teamwork in your relationship. This will allow you both to work together as a team toward common relationship goals, long-term life goals, and more.

Don't Let Empathy Suck You Down a Dangerous Track

Empathy is good, and empathy is important, but don't let it overrule your other emotions so much that it drags you into the emotions of your partner in a negative way. Empathy is often misconstrued as feeling another's emotions at such a deep level that it influences your own emotions. This is not correct, and it is a dangerous view to have.

Empathy is very different from the occurrence of you feeding off the emotions of your partner. This occurs when your emotional empathy gets out of control. This is a very dangerous situation that can lead to codependency. It can make it very hard, also, to support your partner if you are drowning in their emotional influence. If you get roped into their complicated web of emotions, you will not be able to sort through your feelings, let along with theirs. Rather, try to help your partner unravel their web while maintaining a firm and steady, but compassionate, ground. This is where cognitive empathy comes into play. Keep your self-identity intact and use your resolve to help them wade through the waters of whatever they are going through.

Don't get caught up in your own emotions, separate from but influenced mildly by your perception of your partner's, in the process, however. Process your emotions, yes, but try not to confuse them with your partner's specific emotions. If you do, the situation could get misconstrued, and you could jump to conclusions and assumptions and cause a miscommunication that could make the situation worse.

Be attentive. Don't be an emotional crutch, so to speak, but be attentive and support your partner. Attentively and genuinely give your partner the attention that they deserve in a healthy manner, without letting your attention spiral into an alteration of your own mood.

Use Empathic Listening to Validate Your Partner

Empathy helps to validate the emotions of your partner. In order to validate your partner, you need to listen to them. Don't just hear them speak, but actively and attentively listen. Give your partner your full attention, and then if they want you to reply, you can, with compassion and potential advice. Listening sincerely and intently, without interrupting your partner, is a huge sign of respect, and it shows genuine appreciation for your partner as a person.

Listening also helps you truly understand where your partner is coming from, making it much easier to empathize with them. Listen beyond the words and feel the emotions behind those words and the body language your partner portrays. Empathic listening is very strengthening and healthy for your relationship, and it will build a firm foundation for you and your partner.

When following up with your empathic listening, make sure to pay attention to and remember important details from the conversations. Follow up a few hours, days, or weeks later, depending on the situation, so that your partner will know you truly listened. This lets them know that they communicated clearly and accurately to you, and it builds solid trust between the two of you.

Follow up empathic listening with phrases such as these to open the best communication pathways with your partner:

- "Last week you mentioned…and how are you feeling about it this week?"
- "I just wanted to check up with you about what you said to me the other day. Has anything changed?"
- "You seemed upset the other day. How are you feeling now, and can I help in any way?"
- "I remember you said…so is there anything I can do to make things easier for you today?"
- "You sound frustrated. What can I do to make things better for you?"

You can also use more advanced validation techniques, which offer to your partner signs that you understand their feelings more deeply than the fact that you simply listened. Asking how they feel and similar phrases are beneficial, but they are a bit simplistic on the surface. Here are some deeper phrases that show a more in-depth understanding of the emotions that your partner may be feeling:

- "That looks like it took a lot of work and dedication! I am so proud of you, and I'm sure you must feel great for doing such an amazing job!"
- "You have every right to feel the way that you do. I know that I would go insane if I had to deal with a situation like that! You are handling it much better than I would, and that is so great! I'm here for you, and I support how you are handling this."
- "It is completely healthy to feel that way. The hurt you feel is how anyone would feel in that situation, and I am so sorry that this has happened to you."
- "I am so sorry for confusing you the other day. You are right to feel frustrated. I apologize for not understanding your point of view at the time."
- "I understand that you are scared. It would be hard not to be in that position. Is there anything I can do to make you feel safer and to lift your spirits?"

See? This is a lot more in-depth than a phrase such as "I understand that you are anxious about this." It gives an extra layer of understanding. "I understand that you are anxious about this, because I would be too. Being yelled at or belittled is unfair to you, and you have every right to feel upset," is a much more in-depth version of the first phrase. If you are sure that your partner is feeling a certain way, after thoroughly listening to them, then this dialogue, rich in a deeper understanding of the situation, may be a good idea. The identification of the specific emotion, instead of a blanket phrase such as "I'm sorry you are upset," is a great way to reveal that you can pick up on your partner's emotions accurately.

Body Language and Signals

Be mindful of those bodily communication signals we talked about in the first few chapters. Pick up on those signals as best as you can and assess the emotional situation of your partner. Step into their shoes to an extent and find their perspective. That way, you can help them to the best of your ability, and you can come down to their level to meet them eye-to-eye.

Take care to ensure that you do not use this opportunity to look down upon your partner from a higher standing, for this can make your partner feel inferior. It will have a negative effect. Don't use your strength in this position, during a very vulnerable situation for your partner, to get any kind of upper hand or superiority complex. Do not lord over your partner the fact that in this particular situation, you are more emotionally stable. Rather, pick up on their emotions through the use of compassion and empathy and help your partner the best way you can. Empathize with them by being kind and genuine in asking questions, showing your concern, and letting your partner know that you are there for them.

Signals in this situation include things like slumped shoulders, frowns, averted eyes, and crossed arms. Pick up on these signals to determine the next best step, and do not be abrasive or it will just throw them deeper into their negative body language and emotions. Try to get to know your partner well enough through dialogue and compassionate questions so that you will know the signs that they give off. That way, when you see these signs, you can assist and give aid to your partner.

Use your strength in these situations to share it with your partner through support, and give off signals of compassion and not superiority. Give a gentle smile, be open in your body language, and be someone that your partner can fall back on and embrace. Open your eyes and your arms to them, and exude positive emotions and encouragement so that they feel safe and secure in your arms. This will build trust and intimacy. It ties very close, in fact, to what we have talked about thus far regarding trust and respect. If you respect your partner, it will show through the kindness you share in these situations. They will respect you more for it, and trust you in hard situations.

Don't Try to Fix Every Issue

For the truly empathetic, this can be a tough one. When you hear your partner out and feel that they are hurting, it is common to want to try to fix every issue. This can be good, at times, but in many cases your partner needs to be able to sort things out on their own. This helps them build personal strength and character. The best thing you can do is be there for them. Be a shoulder to cry on and an ear to listen. Many people need to open the flood gates and let everything out in order to piece it all together. You don't have to respond in this case, simply listen.

When somebody is deeply distraught, or there are many emotions going on in their head, it is hard to make sense of it. In the turmoil of emotion, many things seem to be spinning into chaos on the inside. When somebody has the opportunity to voice their emotions, it becomes a more tangible thing that can be pieced together. It's easier for people to voice these emotions if there is someone who will listen. That is why many people pay money to a therapist in order to voice their feelings. You can be the stand-in for your partner and allow them the outlet they need to bounce off ideas and emotions. Once they do, it will be easier for them to make sense of the storm inside.

If they speak and ask for advice, you may offer it. Just don't try to jump right in there and offer advice until your partner is ready. They need time to process every side of the issue, and that's ok.

Saying invalidating phrases, however well-intentioned they may be, is a very bad idea. In fact, it is just about the worst thing you can do in a particularly sensitive or negative emotional situation. Here is a list of phrases you should absolutely avoid in these situations, for your and your partner's own wellbeing:

- "That's not true!"
- "This is what you need to do…"
- "Don't worry about it."
- "Hey, it could be worse!"
- "Let it go."
- "Just ignore it!"
- "Someday, it will get better."
- "I feel you, one time this happened to me…"
- A funny joke or sarcastic remark to deflect their emotions

Saying phrases such as the ones above trivializes the emotions of your partner, and that is not what you should do. It is the opposite of empathetic to try to coerce your partner to ignore, push down, or laugh off their emotions. As I said before, your partner needs to feel and work through their emotions. Processing your emotions is emotionally healthy, and it helps you learn from it and overcome it. If you ignore it or push it away, it will never get resolved. Furthermore, turning their problems into a joke makes them feel disrespected and gives off the impression that you were never truly listening in the first place. Tread carefully here, and when in doubt, stay silent and simply listen.

CHAPTER 5
Create Deeper Intimacy

As to not beat around the proverbial bush, we all know that intimacy is closely intertwined with most romantic relationships, and to put it bluntly, people like to have sex. When you tie sexual intimacy into a romantic and steady relationship, however, a deeper level of communication must occur in order for you both to get the most out of the encounter. It will also cultivate the benefit of fostering a closer relationship overall.

Better than sex alone, in your relationship, is the ability to have fulfilling sexual encounters that make you both feel appreciated, closely bonded, and satisfied. The key to this is proper communication in the bedroom. In order for this to occur, you have to both feel that your voice has been heard so that you are both comfortable and feel the best from each sexual encounter. Sex isn't all about the body after all, it's about the experience, and it has a lot to do with the words you both say.

That isn't to say that you don't use your body and non-vocal communication during sex, however. You also have to understand the more subtle forms of sexual communication that go beyond words, such as body language, physical touch, and wordless sounds. We will go into that further in a moment.

Sex involves a lot of give-and-take. It also involves consent, voicing your sexual needs, wants, and aversions, and compromising so that neither you nor your partner feels unsatisfied or frustrated. This all involves proper communication in order to set up boundaries, sexual preferences, and more. You both want your needs to be met, and the best way to accomplish this is to voice your needs and wants openly with your partner and to listen when they voice theirs.

Furthermore, communication outside the bedroom is key to a good sex life within the bedroom. Your partner is much more likely to jump in bed with you if they feel appreciated, validated, listened to, and safe. Trust is a key factor here as well. The ability to trust your partner outside the bedroom will make it so much easier to feel comfortable inside the bedroom. We will go over how communication out of the bedroom transitions into the bedroom in this chapter as well.

Let's go over some ways to get the most out of your sexual communication and cultivate a healthy basis for your sexual encounters in your relationship through communication.

Set Proper Boundaries and Expectations

Consent is key, and it must be given in any and all sexual situations. Once you set up the consensual agreements, start talking about your needs and your wants, comforts, and discomforts, and encourage your partner to do the same so you can have a common ground and a basis for compromise if the situation warrants it. Plus, if you don't get everything out in the open right off the bat when it comes to your mind you will forget it and be sexually displeased. You will also hold off from saying it so long that you will push it down and it will distract you during sex as you are constantly thinking about how much you wish you had voiced it beforehand. It's always better to say what is on your mind regarding sex than to keep it in and cause embarrassment or regret after the fact.

Setting up proper boundaries for sex is a way to protect both yourself and your partner, which is important if you honestly care about yourself and about your partner. Make it clear before you get serious in the relationship about what makes you uncomfortable, what you are ok with, and what is negotiable once you have had time to get comfortable with your partner. Never jump into any sexual encounter, regardless of the length of your relationship, without first setting up these boundaries to protect yourself, your partner, and your relationship. For instance, if you are comfortable kissing, having consensual missionary sex, and participating in foreplay, but are not comfortable with things such as anal sex, bondage, and more adventurous sexual kinks, make that well known before you strip and get down to business. It will save you a lot of embarrassment, discomfort, and frustration in the long run.

In order to be comfortable in your relationship, and to avoid conflict and distress, proper boundaries and expectations for sexual encounters must be discussed. There needs to be a clearly defined divide between what is ok and what crosses a line. Make sure you discuss what makes you uncomfortable and make sure you listen to what makes your partner uncomfortable in order to avoid any negative situations. Also, make sure that you are firm in your decisions if your partner does ever cross a line, that way, confusion will not spiral out of control, and your partner won't get the wrong idea. The best advice I can give you here is to be as honest as you can. Don't let the embarrassment of telling your partner you are not ok with something to overrule your own levels of comfort. It will only make it harder and more embarrassing further down the road.

Next, discuss what both you and your partner want out of the encounter. Voice what makes you feel good and what does not, and set up those guidelines so that you can have the most enjoyable time that you can while your partner feels the same. For example, tell your partner what areas of your body you are comfortable with them touching and which you are not comfortable with. You can also discuss positions you are comfortable with, whether or not certain kinks are ok, and what really gets you fired up.

Then, talk about specifics. What do you want to do during your next sexual encounter? Let your partner know what you are expecting, ask what they want to do, where they want to be touched, and more. Make it sexy, talk about what would curl your toes, where you want to be kissed, what positions would drive you wild, and more. It will make the sex enjoyable, keep your partner interested in what will turn you on, and it will allow you both to get fired up and going without floundering around or scrambling to get to the right spot. You can't read each other's minds, so read each other's lips.

If you talk about the positions you would like to use, where you want to be touched, what kinds of foreplay you would like to perform to get you both hot and bothered, and more, it can really spice up the sex, and it will also boost the sexual tension in the room as you talk through what you are going to do to one another. It will make the whole scenario more pleasurable for the both of you, and you'll both be able to strike while the iron is hot.

Communicate During Intimacy

Now, we all know that the biggest and best part of sex is the physical sensations; however, communication is just as stimulating and just as important. While you are intimate with your partner, it is a good idea to constantly communicate what feels good, what doesn't, and what you are enjoying about your partner. Phrases such as "How does this feel?", "Is this comfortable?", and "Do you like this?" are good starting points.

Furthermore, communicate what you like about what is happening, as this makes your partner feel good and it boosts their confidence if they know that they are doing a good job. You can use verbal or nonverbal communication here, such as a smile, passionate kisses, phrases like "This feels so good", and more to foster this positive communication. Even certain noises give off good communication during a sexual encounter.

Lastly, compliments and sweet words are beneficial during sex. Even building up to it, you can comment on how beautiful, handsome, or sexy your partner is, which will give them confidence and drive once you intertwine. Passionate sex is fueled just as much by ardent words as it is by physical stimulation.

Get Comfortable with the Words

A lot of the time, people avoid talking about sex before doing the act because certain words or phrases make them uncomfortable. This can lead to a bit of a roadblock while discussing and engaging in sexual intercourse because it makes it harder to talk through what is happening. If the words make you uncomfortable, try getting more familiar with them so you can be more comfortable during sex and while talking about it. Voice your discomfort with your partner and talk through this together.

You may even be able to find words to replace the ones that make you uncomfortable so that it will be easier to speak about them. You can try using euphemisms for certain phrases and body parts to minimize confusion and unease. For instance, you can say: "I would like for you to go inside me," instead of saying: "I want to be penetrated" or "I'd like to have vaginal intercourse." Another example could be that you are uncomfortable saying words such as penis, vagina, or anus. You can change these words to something less anatomical or blunt, such as changing penis to erection, member, shaft, or dick or some unique nickname you come up with.

Furthermore, if, after talking it through with your partner and attempting to get comfortable with it, you are still uncomfortable with certain words or phrases, you could use hand gestures or physical communication to get the point across. In the end, whatever makes you most comfortable is the best choice. Being comfortable and relaxed makes sex much more enjoyable for you both, and less awkward.

Use that Body!

Do you remember how we talked about body language and physical communication? This seriously comes into play here with sexual intimacy. The ability for your partner to pick up on sexual and romantic cues will make transitioning into the bedroom, and into sex, a lot more fluid and enjoyable. It's all about giving off the right signals. Your body is its own communication tool, not just your lips and voice. Use your body language and physical touch to create a deep, intimate bond with your partner and feel your way through intimacy in the most sensual, connected way you can. Communicate with touch, feel your partner's body on yours, and use your eyes, lips, mouth, and whatever other parts of yourself that you can to show your partner how you feel! This can be really fun, and it is a very good tactic in the bedroom.

Physical Touch

The most literal use of your body in a sexual encounter is your use of physical touch. Use the power of this sensual form of communication to your advantage and wow your partner while leading them down a path they can easily follow with the right physical cues. Pepper passionate kisses on your partner's body to show just how eager you are to appreciate their body. Kiss their neck to insinuate you are in the mood, get them fired up, and let them know you want the same treatment right back! You can even be direct and, with your partner's consent, place your hand on their erogenous zones or their hand on yours. Raise the temperature of your sexual passion by making it impossible for your partner to miss what your intentions are! Act like love-struck teens again and play footsies, wink at them, and plant a sultry kiss on your partner's lips. I'm sure your partner will get the message really quick! If they don't, there are other ways to get your partner's attention! More on that next.

Body Language

Body language can either dampen the heat of romance or spice it up! Turning your body away from your partner, for instance, or lying in a closed-off position, can give off the vibe that you don't want to be touched. Biting your lip and staring your partner up and down, however, can give them the signal that you are ready for some kissing action. It's all in the subtle ways that you portray yourself to your partner. Something as simple as a smile, even, can make you seem open and inviting to your partner. Use your body to your advantage to give off the best signals to your partner, even if they are indirect. It will show you just how much your partner pays attention to you, and how closely bonded you are if you notice that they pick up on your innuendos.

Some common body language signs we show during intimacy, even if we don't realize it at the time, are as simple as closing your eyes during a pleasurable experience, arching your back during enjoyable intercourse, grasping the sheets uncontrollably to ground yourself as your world is shaken by the feeling of your partner's body on yours, and parting your lips slightly in ecstasy.

More bold or conscious forms of body language communication during intimacy are commonplace as well, and we are more aware of the fact that we do them. When you turn your head a certain way to expose your neck to your partner, for instance, it shows that you are letting your walls down and opening yourself up to your partner. It also indicates vulnerability and trust as you send off a signal that you want to be kissed all over your body and that you want them to come closer, possibly. Even the way you glance at your partner, wink, smile, and turn your body toward them shows undeniable invitations that you want them to come closer to you.

If all else fails, you can always be more direct in how you communicate your sexual desires. If you are in the mood for a hot and steamy interaction, you can always tease your partner by walking toward the bedroom and leaning against the doorframe in a provocative way. You can also unbutton your shirt, expose skin, and run your hands down your body while mimicking sexually pleasing movements. If that does not catch their eye, there is always the option of undressing and coyly showing off that body as you walk away. They will probably come after you like a dog after a bone!

Sound

The right sounds can make your intimacy heat up faster than the next gasp that escapes your lips. Wordless noises can say as much, if not more, than any words you can speak to your partner. It is a primal form of communication that can turn on your partner, lead them to all the right places, and communicate just what you are feeling. For instance, an involuntary moan when your partner touches and kisses just the right spot can make a passionate moment turn into a symphony of pleasure. Making small noises when your partner kisses you in certain places can unlock a fervent part of their brain that can raise your intimacy to the next level. Show your partner how you feel and let your lips release all the signs they need to know that you are enjoying their actions. These sounds communicate emotions, intentions, sensations, and so much more. So, soundproof that room and make your own sensual music with your partner until the sun rises.

Use your natural sexual sounds to egg your partner on and create a more fervent bedroom environment. Give your partner positive feedback as they pleasure you so that without having to look up from what they are doing, they can hear your pleasure like music to their ears. Don't hold back your moans, sighs, heavy breathing, and your little squeaks of pleasure, because it is a natural way through which we communicate how much we enjoy the moment when our lips and brains are busy elsewhere. Just let it flow out as naturally as the sensations flowing over your skin, through your nerves, and in your core. If you do it often enough, and it turns your partner on, you may get to hear some happy noises from them as well!

Try Not to Jump to Conclusions

Jumping to the wrong conclusions can cause your partner to jump right out of bed. Communicate during sex, and do not simply assume your partner's needs and wants. This is where consent comes in, as well as what you two have discussed about what you expect and what you would like or dislike in the bedroom. When in doubt, ask your partner! Sex is not a silent act, as many people know.

If you assume what your partner wants and just go for it without talking it through, you can leave them unsatisfied and come out feeling like a fool. When in doubt, always ask questions and communication throughout a sexual encounter. It is always better to ask than to assume. It doesn't have to be complicated, either. Simply ask: "Is this ok?" or "Does this feel good?", and your partner will be able to openly communicate what they need, want, and like. You can be content knowing that you have done everything that they have voiced wanting you to do, and that you have not crossed any lines. This can build trust and respect, and if they are happy, they will likely reciprocate and show you the same respect.

Let Your Partner Know That You Appreciate Them

Compliments are a wonderful way to heat up the mood, and it makes sex more fluid and enjoyable when the self-confidences of the people involved are lifted. Sweet nothings, passionate talks outside and inside the bedroom, body language as you look your partner over, and more really shows your partner how much they mean to you and how affected you are by their presence.

Partners tend to appreciate each other's bodies more if they feel appreciated on the inside. An intimate relational bond between two partners is heavily influenced by how they feel for one another. Before you enter the bedroom, always resolve any conflicts you have and make sure your partner knows how you feel in a non-sexual way. This will uplift spirits, sex drives, and affection for one another in the long run.

Another way to appreciate your partner before and after sex is to do sweet things for them throughout the day. It will warm them up to you, make them feel appreciated, and communicate how much you care for them. It is not directly linked to sex, but it improves your relationship and may lead to them showing how much they appreciate *you* in bed if you know what I mean. Communicating in sweet ways to your partner is a great way to improve and strengthen your relationship, and it is really nice to show them a bit of love every once in a while, in a way that isn't sexual. It lets them know that sex is not the only thing on your mind, yet it will translate well into the bedroom as you both learn to love and support one another. You can also do sweet, appreciative things for your partner that can lead to the bedroom, such as a nice massage, a trail of flower petals to the bed, draw them a nice hot bath, pour them a glass of wine, light some candles for them, and more. This is a great way to make your partner feel cared for while enticing them to reciprocate in the bedroom.

Be Open to New Things

Being adventurous and bouncing new and exciting ideas off one another in the bedroom is a great way to spice up the relationship and keep it alive. Spontaneity, within the realms of your agreed upon consensual boundaries, is very exciting and is its own stimulating form of intimate dialogue. As we discussed, communication is not only verbal. A bit of surprise and imagination through your physical touch communicates new and exciting areas of your intimate relationship that you may have never known were there.

Examples of new things you can try as a couple include:
- Sex positions (i.e., missionary, cowgirl, doggy-style, wheelbarrow,
- Toys (i.e., vibrators, butt plugs, etc.)
- Role-play (i.e., student and professor, little red riding hood and the big bad wolf, naughty wife and plumber, vampire and victim, etc.)
- Watching sexy movies or pornography together to get ideas
- Sexy talk/dirty talk

- Food play (i.e., ice cream, chocolate syrup, whipped cream, maple syrup, etc.)
- Temperature play (safely)
- Change power roles (i.e., dominant versus submissive)
- Foreplay techniques
- Tantric sex
- Light bondage (i.e., silk scarves, fuzzy handcuffs, etc.)
- Mutual masturbation
- Anal sex
- Turning the lights off or dimming them
- Playing sexy music
- Massage with soothing oils
- Move outside the bedroom (i.e., kitchen table, floor, couch, shower, etc.)
- Read the Kama Sutra
- Make a personal sex tape (Just don't distribute it!)
- And more!

Ask, and You Shall Receive

Ask your partner for what you want out of the sexual encounter so they can please you without reading your mind. You can even do it in a sexy way by pleading with sultry whispers in your partner's ear, biting your lip and sliding your hands over your body where you want to be touched, and more. Drive your partner crazy so that there is no room for them to say no, and you can fall head over heels for each other in bed when the time comes.

Communication as a Sexual Guidance Tool

Use communication to guide your partner through your sexual encounters. You can even role-play a bit here and act as your partner is brand new to all of this. If they are ok with it, you can role-play that your partner is still a virgin and that you are the teacher showing them the ropes. Whatever way you choose, guidance is imperative, and it can be very sexy. For your partner to know how to please you, and vice versa, you have to be able to communicate your specific needs and desires. Phrases that are associated with this during sex include: "more", "over here", "go down a bit", "faster", "slower", "harder", "softer", and more.

Guide and show your partner what you want and exactly how you want it. It can turn them on and make the situation fun as you guide each other through pleasurable moments. You can even take your partner's hand and move it to where you want to be touched. Use your own hand and do on them what you want to be done to yourself, or you can even touch yourself to tease them and get them eager to bat your hand to the side and go to town.

Start Outside the Bedroom

The best way to get the most out of your intimate relationship is to start outside the bedroom. Build up to it. Tease and entice your partner with subtle touches, whispered sweet nothings, sneak peeks into what is to be expected once the time comes for you to intertwine, and discussions about what will make you both happy in the bedroom.

You can also start the sexual tension outside of the bedroom. Tease your partner by leaving a trail of clothing to the bedroom. Start with the shirt, the pants, the underwear, and at the end of the clothing rainbow will be you, in all of your glory! You can also leave little suggestive notes around the house, send naughty pictures and messages, and more! Gentle dirty talk throughout the day is a good tactic, too, but only if you think your partner will be ok with it. Building up the sexual tension throughout the day is a great way to get your partner ready to pounce when the time comes! Do just enough to give your partner a sneak peek and leave them begging for the main course.

Another important factor of out-of-bedroom communication that feeds into bedroom time is the establishment of trust and supportive communication. If throughout your relationship, in non-sexual situations, you have maintained relationship stability and respectful communication, that respect you hold for one another, the comfort you share in each other, and the attraction you will have built up will lead to a much more enjoyable encounter in intimate situations. If you have a rocky relationship full of arguments, distrust, and anger outside of the bedroom, it won't magically translate into a passionate and enjoyable sex life despite what some movies and books portray.

Make sure your communication separate from intimate communication is stable first before you build upon your intimacy. It will make you both feel more loved, more comfortable, and more compatible in the bedroom if you do.

CHAPTER 6
Gain Healthy Conflict Resolution In Your Relationship And Mend Bridges

As we discussed earlier in this book, conflict resolution is imperative for the stability of a relationship. Point-blank, if a relationship is rocky and full of resentment and anger, it will crumble and fall apart over time. Every time a conflict is not resolved, a hairline fracture sneaks into the foundation of your relationship, and the pressure of all of the suppressed emotions will cause that foundation to crack and break loose. In this chapter, I'm going to show you how to prevent this from happening and how to mend that foundation with proper communication techniques and advice.

We've gone over how to resolve any conflict, but how about preventing conflict from occurring? What about the aftermath of conflict? Well, now that we know how to resolve a conflict, let's figure out how to repair those broken pieces after the fact. We'll also come up with some good ways to prevent the conflict from even starting. Let's get started, shall we?

How to Prevent Conflict

Conflict prevention is essential in a relationship, and it is just as essential as conflict resolution. When you stop a conflict from happening, in a healthy way, you won't have to fix the emotional trauma later on down the road. We're going to go over some concrete ways to help you prevent future conflicts and strengthen your communication with your partner.

Don't Always Try to Be Right.

Getting in the last word may give you instant gratification. Feeling that you are always right and that you know everything may make you happy at the moment, but I promise you it won't make you happy in the long-run. Being arrogant enough to think that you can never be wrong is like taking the fast-track into a single-town. You will never be able to resolve anything, never be able to discuss anything with your partner, and never be able to grow as a couple.

Relationships are all about to give and take. Your partner has to be right sometimes, and you are going to be wrong sometimes. You have to learn to accept that if you want to have a healthy relationship. If you don't, it will only lower your self-esteem over time and severely harm your partner. If your partner feels like they are always wrong, it will make them feel bad, and it will also cause a lot of frustration. You can not be right all of the time, and that is ok. You have to accept that you may have faults, but that does not have to be a bad thing. You can work as a team with your partner and overcome those faults together. If you overcome them, you can grow and learn from your mistakes.

If you truly care for your partner, know that you don't have to be right all the time. The person you choose to be with is someone you should love, and if you really love them, you appreciate who they are and know that they are smart enough to understand what is going on most of the time. Don't degrade your partner and assume that they are never right, because if that is true, and your partner is never right, what is the point of being in that relationship in the first place? Understand that coming to a compromise, standing on common ground, and accepting defeat at times are much more positive and enlightening than being stubborn. Reach conclusions together as a team, and stand together to overcome issues in your relationship. Strengthen that bond, which is so important in a relationship, and it will make you feel so much happier. I guarantee it.

Look at it this way: Would you want your partner to patronize you? Belittle you? Make you feel like you are never right, and that you are not smart? I don't believe you would. Therefore, don't do the same to your partner, who you care about. Take a second and empathize. See the issue from their perspective, and try to realize where they are coming from. Neither of you can be right all the time, and I'm not saying you are wrong all of the time, but there is a balance that must be maintained. Just talk things out with your partner and try to fix things together, instead of making every discussion a battle, and you will both come out much happier and prevent arguments.

Prevent Issues, but Don't Ignore Issues

We are talking about preventing heated, aggressive arguments in this chapter. We are not discussing how to avoid confrontation entirely. When there is an issue, it needs to be brought to light and handled with maturity, proper communication, and respect. Prevent the frustration and abrasion while discussing the root issue that is bothering you, and don't attack your partner. Work as a team, grow together, and never push things away out of fear or embarrassment, or they will never be resolved. Even little things build up over time, so it's best to nip them in the bud before that happens! Eliminate the possibility of misunderstandings and blown gaskets!

If you don't confront the issue, you will slowly boil inside and burst like a pressurized pot of water, harming your relationship with your partner in potentially irreversible ways. Take the time to think things through and present your thoughts to your partner without fear. If you truly trust your partner, there is no need to fear their reaction anyway! Communication is always better than silence, and your partner will trust and respect you more if you are open and honest with them. Take this as an opportunity to strengthen your bond and grow closer as a team while you tackle tough issues together!

Choose Your Battles Wisely

If you nit-pick and harbor resentment after every little thing your partner does wrong, it will cause a problem. Your partner will grow distant and less likely to come to you with issues if they fear that you will only respond with anger and aggravation. Let the small things slide off your back, and try to confront the bigger things that truly affect your relationship so you can remain close and more than tolerate one another.

For example, an issue you should let roll off your back would be something like your partner deciding that they'd rather fold clothes than roll them up. Yeah, maybe it's annoying, but at the end of the day, the clothes still get put up. Don't nag your partner when they are just trying to help. It may not be exactly the way you would do it, but that's ok. They are still putting in the effort, which is what matters.

Now, if it's a big issue like your partner neglecting their promises or cheating on you, then yeah, you can express a fair amount of anger. No one would blame you for that, just resolve it in a mature way. The little things, however, are not going to matter a week from now, or a year, or ten years. Avoid inflicting lasting damage over something that is fleeting and unrelated to your relationship in the long-run. Choose your battles, be empathetic, and let yourself relax every once in a while. It will turn out ok, I promise.

Don't Project Personal or Unrelated Problems onto Your Partner.

One of the most harmful things you can do is project negative emotions onto your partner or blame them for issues unrelated to them. This is not to say you can't confide in your partner, but I'm talking about those times when you are just so frustrated with the day that you snapped at your partner when they did nothing wrong. If you are upset and feel like you are about to snap, excuse yourself and walk away for a bit to calm down. Your partner is there for you. They will comfort you, support you, and love you, so don't push them away or hurt them just because you are hurt. Take responsibility for your own emotions and respect your partner's wellbeing by letting your anxieties and frustrations cool down before you let them loose on someone who only wants to help. If you don't, it will cause those fractures in your relationship that we discussed. If you turn your partner into an unnecessary enemy or a target for negative emotions, it will only lead to a negative outcome for your relationship. Embrace your partner, express your feelings, and let them in. Let your walls down, and that pent-up frustration will subside. Then, you can sort through the emotions that are struggling to escape and strike out at anyone within arm's reach.

Projection is a defense mechanism, but it doesn't have to be! Instead of diverting your emotions to your partner to lessen their effects on you, use your partner as support and let your walls down. Express your emotions, but don't lash out. This will make it impossible for your partner to help and support you because you will likely hurt them and make them get angry right back at you. Tell your partner how you are feeling, apologize if you do catch yourself projecting, and heal together.

Another good mechanism to use in order to avoid projection is to identify the cause of your feelings before you project them onto your partner. Also, take responsibility for your own insecurities and realize that your partner does not deserve to share the burden of your emotions. You don't want to wish negative emotions onto someone you care about, do you? Instead, let them help you, and work through it together so that you feel better and your partner does not get hurt in the crossfire.

Don't Push Down Your Emotions.

If you suppress your emotions, you either become numb to them or explode over time. This is not healthy for you or your relationship. Always communicate your emotions to your partner, or let them out in another healthy way, to prevent snapping at them and causing aggression. When you work together as a team to resolve an issue or find a healthy outlet to release the pressure of your emotions, you will become stronger as a person, stronger as a couple, and you will not grow to resent your partner over ill-expressed issues and misunderstandings.

When you suppress your feelings, it also can make your partner feel unimportant or unappreciated. They may feel that you have grown distant, and you do not trust them enough to open up to them and confide in their comfort and love. Your partner is there for you with open arms. They should be your rock, your support, and your confidence. If you can't let your walls down and express your emotions to them, it can make them feel unneeded and useless as a partner. When you are in a relationship, you become a team, and part of being a team involves helping one another and being honest. If you can be honest and expressive with your partner, you can build your trust and tackle anything together!

Furthermore, suppressing your emotions can build stress up in your mind, and it can cause negative outcomes for your body. When you stress, you release cortisol, which can wreak havoc on your energy levels, blood pressure, anxiety levels, heart rate, and more. When you start to feel bad, it can make it harder to control the emotions you are pushing down, creating pressure, and fracturing you mentally, emotionally, and physically. This will translate badly into your relationship, and you don't want that. Let your emotions out in a healthy way, so they don't cause problems in your relationship. Let them out in a calm way, and they will not escape from your grasp and cause damage in every area of your life, including your relationships.

If you have to, it is perfectly ok to let your emotions out on someone other than your partner, as long as you make sure they know that you are ok and that you are not avoiding them due to anger. There are a lot of ways to express and release emotions in a healthy way, and none of these ways are wrong! Anything you can do to calm down is ok, and your way may be different than your partner's. That is ok! Your outlets for emotional release may even be different than my examples, and you know what? That is ok too.

For some basis on what I mean, I will give you some examples of ways you can express and release your pent-up emotions. Walk outside and scream at the sky. Scream into a pillow. Heck, punch a pillow if you need to! Just don't direct that energy at your partner, and don't push it down so far inside you that you explode. Let it all out, and I promise you will feel better. Cry, scream, go on a walk, write it all down and throw it away, blaring heavy metal music, or vent it all out to your favorite stuffed animal. There are so many options there for you, and many that are unique and can only be discovered by you! The important thing is that you are comfortable and that your emotions get out there so you can process them. Anything you can do to prevent a negative fallout, without causing damage or harm to yourself or others, do it. It's ok. It's valid. It's natural. Whatever you do, if it makes you feel better, is perfectly validated. Just don't ignore those emotions, and don't hurt yourself or anyone else.

Don't Speak or Act on Impulse.

Try to think through everything you do or say before you act on it. If you speak from raw emotion, your heart could be overruling your head. Give your brain a moment to catch up and process the emotions so you can piece together a response that will allow for open communication. You want to be able to address the issue with your partner while working together to resolve it. If you jump in with guns blazing, you probably won't get the results or the solution you need. This is the same with actions, regardless of the emotion or urge involved.

When you act on impulse, you also leap right over the boundaries, consent, expectations, trust, and respect that you have cultivated with your partner. This can lead to hurt, frustration, distrust, fear, and so much more. It is not fair to your partner to assume that what you want to do is ok, and just because you are angry, turned on, upset, sad, or experiencing any emotion and following your gut reactions does not make it right. Always take your partner into consideration before you do anything, and don't neglect the promises and expectations you have established together. That is a quick way to destroy any bond you have formed with your partner because you are dismissing the respect you have for your partner, and that can appear very inconsiderate.

Let me be clear here about what I mean regarding impulse. By impulse, I do not mean kissing your partner out of the blue, buying a gift that you just immediately know your partner will love or surprising your partner with something you know they will appreciate. I'm not talking about positive relationship instincts. What I mean by acting on impulse is crossing lines by acting on pure emotion without proper thought or consideration. For example, it is not considerate to say something mean out of anger without thinking, or to strike your partner out of anger, or to force your partner to do something just because you want to, right then, at that moment, regardless of their feelings. Don't let your emotions or desires overrule those of your partner, especially regarding the boundaries that you know for sure are set in stone. This can lead to serious, irreversible consequences.

Acting on impulse can lead to many misunderstandings, lots of confusion, heaps of hurt, a plethora of arguments, and so much more in a relationship. Take control of your impulses and strengthen both yourself and your relationship. Show your partner the trustworthiness and consideration they deserve. If you don't, your relationship will suffer, your partner may lose trust in you, and you will lose control over your own actions. Try to avoid this at all costs, unless you are absolutely sure it will not hurt your partner or relationship. When in doubt, speak up and ask your partner before doing or saying anything on impulse.

Take Proper Care of Yourself

Last but definitely not least, take care of yourself. Taking care of yourself is imperative for fostering healthy relationship communication, and it will prevent future conflicts. It is not selfish to take care of yourself, either. It is necessary! Eat nutritious meals, get enough sleep, and make sure you pay attention to your needs and emotions. All of these factor into your mood and wellbeing as a whole and this directly translates into your relationship. If you don't take care of yourself, you will feel grumpy, have low self-esteem, and much more. These negative factors can lead to frustration, which can bleed into your relationship and cause arguments, hurt, and misdirected anger.

Take care of yourself in order to take care of your relationship, and take care of your partner as well. All of these factor into a healthy relationship, healthy mindsets, and healthy bodies. If you and your partner are well taken care of, you will communicate and interact in a much more positive way!

How to Pick Up the Pieces and Mend Bridges Together

Let's say you didn't listen to my advice about preventing an argument. Maybe you slipped up and need to find a way to reconcile your relationship. Whatever the reason, you are in the right place! Picking up the pieces after an argument is just as important as resolving the argument itself, and I am here to help you learn just how to do that. Let's go over some of the ways you can heal the wounds caused by arguments and become closer as a couple.

Give Your Partner Space

Don't abandon your partner, but after an argument, you both need a little space and time. Give your partner, and yourself, that brief period where you can disconnect with the situation physically so that you can focus on it mentally. Simply go and sit in a separate room for a few minutes while your partner does the same. Cool down, reflect, and process what has occurred. This will give you both time to think things over and embrace forgiveness.

Take care when doing this, however. Do not blatantly ignore your partner if they seem as though they still need to talk, and make sure you make it clear that you are leaving the room so you can both calm down. If they think you are storming off in anger, giving the silent treatment, or ignoring the situation, it can give off the wrong impression and cause friction. Take all the space and time both of you need, but make it clear that you are doing it to cool off and process what has happened.

Don't Resort to Make-Up Sex.

Going along with the above point, don't immediately fly into bed for make-up sex. That is never a good idea. Just as negative prods at your partner right after an argument are bad, positive distractions are bad too for similar reasons. If you leap back into intimacy right after an argument, it will distract your partner, and neither you nor they will be able to properly process their emotions. It will get thrown out the window in lieu of quick sexual gratification.

Additionally, having sex after an argument can feel a bit hollow, and it can start a pattern of sex for the sake of sex and take out the deeper intimacy and emotional connection that you need to be able to share in such an encounter. When you jump into make-up sex instead of healthy space and dialogue, it will take out an important communicative step as well, which is never a good idea. Your best bet is to wait a while, calm down, and don't mistake the heat of passion and anger for the urge to have sex.

Learn from Your Mistakes and Apply it to the Future.

If you were the reason for the argument, and you've apologized sincerely, back up your words with actions. Make it your goal to do better next time and not repeat the action that caused the issue. Learn from your mistakes and grow as a person so your relationship will become stronger. Take every failure and turn it into a building block of knowledge that you can pour into the foundation of your relationship.

Don't Beat Yourself Up About the Argument.

Everyone argues. It's natural, and at times it's good so you can get your thoughts and emotions out there. Having small conflicts actually builds the character of a relationship, so don't feel guilty if you have one with your partner. Just try to go over the steps I gave you for preventing further arguments, and you will be fine! Just make sure to sincerely apologize to your partner after a conflict, and make sure you let them know how much you appreciate them. Don't beat yourself up about it. It's ok!

Don't Negate the Resolution of the Argument.

Once a conflict is resolved, leave it. Do not go back minutes or hours later, and try to re-justify what you said or did. This negates anything you have said before, and it breaks down the trust of the relationship. Once a conflict is resolved and done with, there is no need to go back and add extra bits of dialogue that will just flare it all back up again to cover your own behind. Leave the argument in the past, accept what you did wrong, and move on.

CHAPTER 7
Tips For Talking About Difficult Topics

In any relationship, there are going to be some tough situations and difficult topics that are going to be brought up. These heavy conversations aren't often happily anticipated, but they are necessary. We're going to go over what these conversations could be, tips on how to handle and address them, and why we should not avoid these important but difficult conversations.

Difficult Topics Many People Have to Face During Their Relationships

There is a wide variety of topics that people find difficult in their daily lives and relationships, and it is different for everyone. However, I'm going to highlight some of the most difficult roadblocks people come upon in their relationships so you can get an idea for the types of difficult topics I am referring to in my advice throughout this chapter. As I said, there are many more difficult topics that are not covered here, but the ones I've listed are ones that many people can relate to across the board.

Loss

Loss of a loved one is likely the most difficult situation in anyone's life. Therefore, it can be very hard to talk about. The key here is to be absolutely considerate of your partner if they are going through loss and be there to support them. It can be difficult to know what to say in these situations, and sometimes silence is best, but try to let your partner know how much you care about them and that you are there whenever they need you. Discussing feelings after a loss can be really hard, but it is a big part of the overall healing process.

Sexual Consent

Sexual consent is one of the more awkward topics we talk about in our relationships, but it is something we all must discuss for our own health, emotional wellbeing, and the stability of our relationships. Sexual consent conversations include but are not limited to: the use of protection and contraceptives, discussions about STI disclosure, the desire for whether or not to have children, the limits of sex positions, bondage, hard limits, exclusivity, and more. In order to have a good relationship, these discussions must take place for your safety and comfort in sexual situations.

In-Laws

If you are married, in-laws are definitely going to come into the picture. This can be difficult at times, because you may feel like you are coming between your spouse and their family, or you may feel as though they are struggling to choose between you or their family. This power struggle between you and your spouse's family can put a big strain on your relationship, and discussing your anxieties about this may seem overwhelming. Don't fear your partner's reaction during these conversations and try to be as open and honest as you can be without pointedly attacking their family. It's a fine line that is hard to learn to walk, but if you discuss your in-laws with your spouse openly, it will turn out all right.

Betrayal

We don't like to think it will happen to us, but betrayal can sometimes occur in a relationship. When this happens, your trust in your partner is fragile, you start questioning the relationship, and negative emotions start to stir. It can be really difficult to talk about this topic with your partner, because you may feel incredibly hurt and angry, but you have to if you want to mend the relationship. If your partner has betrayed your trust and you no longer wish to be with them, that is your call, but it is always a good idea to talk it out first and at least gain closure about the situation. Your emotions in this instant are entirely valid, but be the better person and hear what they have to say. You will probably feel better if you do.

Money Problems

Money problems happen; it's just a natural speed bump in life. When they happen, however, you may feel stressed, embarrassed, and a number of other negative emotions. Instead of pushing those feelings away to hide your embarrassment from your partner, it is a good idea to reach out to them for support during that difficult time. They will likely be able to walk you through your issues and help you through your struggles. As a team, it's always best to work these things through together. Don't let your fear of embarrassment, tension, or argument keep you from being truthful about your finances or your feelings.

Sickness and Other Health Issues

You may be embarrassed to talk about your health to your partner, but it is something you must do. If you hide your health issues from your partner, it will hurt your health, fracture the trust of the relationship, and make it impossible for your partner to help you through it and support you. I know sickness and health problems can be scary, but that is what your partner is there for! If you are in it for the long-run, you will want them to know what is ailing you so they can help you every step of the way. You are not a burden to them, and if they truly care, they are absolutely going to want to make sure you are ok above all else.

Past Relationships

Ok, this is a big one. Most people do not want to bring up their past relationships because it can be very embarrassing, emotional, and awkward. It may also make your partner feel as though you are comparing them to an ex. Sometimes, however, it is important to discuss your past with your partner so that they will understand if certain insecurities pop up. If you discuss those insecurities with your partner, then if something makes you uncomfortable, they will know it is not because of them but because of a traumatic experience in your past. It will also help you both learn from past mistakes so you can strengthen your relationship and rise above the unhealthy ones from your past. Open up to your partner in the right way, and it will strengthen your bond. You can talk about past abusive relationships, distrustful ones, triggers, and the like, but here are some things that should be avoided for the health of your relationship: sex life, pet peeves, physical features, favorite date spots, songs that remind you of an ex, etc. It is good to talk about exes in some regards, just make sure to tread lightly and be smart about it.

How to Handle Difficult Conversations

Problem Solve and Tackle it Like a Team.

The most important tip I can give you is to handle difficult situations as a team. If you try to be right all the time or figure things out together, it can make your partner feel useless or like they are not a true part of the team. Work together to tackle these difficult topics so you can overcome things as a unit and grow together. It will strengthen your relational bonds, make it easier to tackle similar situations in the future and prevent your relationship from slowly fracturing over time. Remember, it's all about fixing the issue at hand and not one-upping your partner, especially in sensitive situations. Don't offer unwarranted advice or negate the comments that your partner makes. Instead, lean on one another and fight every battle as a team.

Be Positive

It is very important to remain positive during a difficult situation. If you start making negative comments or retreating from an issue, it can cause stress, frustration, sadness, depression, and more that will cause the situation to spiral out of control. Take a deep breath, keep a level head, and try to be optimistic about the outcome of any situation you may have to face with your partner. In the end, if you want the situation to turn out ok, you have to believe that it will be so. Use compassion, smile, let yourself believe that things will get better, and lean on your partner. You can get through this; you just have to try! Express gratitude at the strength the both of you have for even bringing up the topic, and admire each other's courage. Thank one another for their courage, even. Pep yourself and your partner up and be strong, and you will know that you can tackle anything the world can throw at the two of you!

Don't Put Your Walls Up.

Shutting down during difficult conversations and putting your walls up makes it very difficult for your partner to reach your level, understand what is going on, and help you tackle it. This can make it ten times harder to overcome adversity, and it is not healthy for you, your partner, or your relationship. Trust your partner and let your walls down. Express those emotions you are trying to hide and work through every situation together. You don't have to do this alone. That is what partnership is all about. You have to be trusting and vulnerable so you can navigate those difficult waters together. Be open and honest with these difficult subjects, and it will make all of the smaller things so much easier. If you can open up to your partner and get through the hardest relationship conversations together, you can do anything! What is there to fear?

Utilize Empathy

Empathy and compassion are imperative during difficult situations. If things are rocky, it makes it a lot easier to navigate the situation if you are both open to seeing one another's perspectives and emotions so that you know how to tread carefully. Listen intently to your partner's words during difficult conversations, because you know it must have been hard for them to bring it up in the first place, and they care about you enough to open up and trust you with the situation. Understanding this concept is the first step to take. Then, make sure you give your full attention and remain invested throughout the entire conversation. Don't check out just because the conversation makes you uncomfortable or embarrassed. If your partner trusts you enough to bring the subject up, it is important enough for you to at least listen and offer support. Discuss the issue with your heart and lovingly find a solution together.

Give it All the Time it Needs

Don't skimp and speed through difficult conversations just because it feels uncomfortable. This is degrading the importance of the topic, and it can make your partner feel that you are disinterested and uncaring of the situation. Additionally, choose the time for you to approach your partner wisely. Don't bombard your partner with it right as they walk through the door, just to get it out of the way. Choose a calm, stable time during which to discuss difficult topics to make sure that you are both on level ground. If you do it during an abrupt or busy time of day, the issue will not be resolved in a conclusive fashion, and you will be right back to square one. Make sure to discuss this with your partner, and ensure that you are both in a good enough place to start a conversation regarding the subject. Ask your partner "Is this a good time to talk?," "Can we discuss something that has been on my mind?", "Are you feeling well enough to discuss something important right now?" "I need some help. Do you have a minute for us to sit and talk?" and "When would you be comfortable discussing this issue?" to feel out the environment and pick the best time.

Stay Focused on the Issue and Don't Divert from the Conversation.

The best thing to do during a difficult conversation is to stay on track. If you veer off during a difficult conversation, it won't get resolved when it needs to. It is best to resolve a difficult situation in one sitting so that it won't get brushed under the rug later on down the road. Embrace your courage and see each topic the whole way through to strengthen your relationship and your overall communication abilities. Stay on topic, and try to keep your partner on the same page as well. This will help you both grow in your dialogue and in your relationship. If your partner begins to get off-topic, gently nudge them back on track with phrases such as "That is a great point, but let's see if we can resolve this first. Then, we'll tackle our next step!", or "Let's handle one thing at a time so we can give it the attention it deserves!" These positive phrases will avoid the issue of your partner feeling unheard, and it will keep the current dialogue on track.

Maintain Your Composure

It's easy to get a bit emotional during a difficult conversation, and that is understandable. However, don't let your emotions take control and get out of hand, or it can make it more difficult to talk about the situation. If you need to, you can take a small break and calm down, but don't let your emotions drive the path of the conversation. Try to remain calm and focus on the task at hand. Don't necessarily push away your emotions, because that can be dangerous, but don't let them overrule your mind while trying to resolve that is making you emotional. Additionally, try your best not to raise your voice or let yourself fall into a negative mindset. These can derail the dialogue and stimulate tension and aggression where it doesn't need to be. Talk yourself through these emotions, and express them to your partner so they can keep you on track. You can say, "I'm starting to feel a bit overwhelmed. Can you help me calm down for a few minutes, then we can get back on track? Thank you." This gives you both a moment to pause, collect yourselves, and continue in a constructive way.

Go from Harder to Easier

When you attack a difficult subject, try to go at it from the top down to make it a much easier, fluid conversation. If you start out with the most upsetting or difficult part of a conversation, the rest will flow out much easier and get resolved much faster. Create a dialogue with your partner and think things through. Pinpoint the root cause of the issue, or the most difficult part, and discuss it with your partner. Use phrases such as, "Here is the issue. What do you think we should tackle first?" "What are you having the most trouble with regarding this subject?" "What is bothering you most about what we are about to discuss?" and "What scares you most about this topic?". By zeroing in on the hardest parts of a discussion, you can tackle it head-on as a team and knock it right out of the park! This makes the whole situation easier to resolve and less intimidating in the long-run.

Remove Distractions

Make it harder for you and your partner to get off track by eliminating common distractions. Set your phones on silent mode, for instance, so the dialogue does not get derailed by a text message or phone call. You can always respond to them later, but your relationship is more important at this time. Turn off the television, so you don't veer off into a seemingly easier environment. Turn the radio off as music can alter the ambiance of a room. Make every effort you can to focus on the task at hand and highlight its importance to you and your partner.

Don't Deflect or Minimize Your Partner's Emotions.

Your emotions, as well as your partner's, are valid and justified in every way during a conversation. The worst thing you can do is deflect away from these emotions. Validate your partner's emotions and tackle the root of their cause so you will both feel better after a conversation. Deflecting these emotions can make your partner feel sad, unimportant, and uncared for. This is the opposite of what should occur during a situation because you both want to remain as positive as you can during difficult times. Avoid, at all costs, phrases such as "Grow up," "Everyone feels that way, what makes you any different?" "You'll get over it," "You're dragging me down," "Just ignore it," "Feel this way instead," "Stop being so upset!" and "It's silly to feel that way." These phrases can damage the self-esteem and emotional stability of your partner, so it is best not to say them at all during a sensitive conversation. Instead, be your partner's shoulder to cry on, their rock, and their confidant. Let them know that you hear them, you understand their pain, and that you are there to help in any way that you can.

Don't Give Direct Advice, but Phrase it as a Question.

Instead of telling your partner what to do, when there is no way you know exactly how they are feeling or handling a situation, suggest resolutions in the form of a question. For instance, say: "Would it help if you did this?" instead of "You should do this because I know it will be the best solution," or "This is what you need to do." Other beneficial phrases include: "Do you want to try this together to see if it helps?" "Would you mind if I suggest a possible solution?" "How would you feel if we tried it this way?" "Can I give you a few possible choices, and we can choose one together to see if it works?" and "Would you like to try this with me and see if it helps?" Phrasing things as a question is a great way to offer advice while giving your partner the power to choose instead of feeling like they aren't good enough to choose for themselves how to handle their emotions. If you tell them what to do in an emotional situation, it could just backfire and make those emotions flare. In any situation, it is best to ask your partner how they feel about something before suggesting that they try it for themselves.

Why You Should Not Avoid Difficult Conversations

When there is a difficult discussion that must be bad, don't ignore it. Pushing the topic away is the most detrimental thing you can do in your relationship. By tackling the most difficult discussions together, your relationship will grow and blossom and strengthen so much. Don't let yourself be overruled by anxiety or uncomfortable feelings, because it may cause you to avoid the situation entirely if you get too scared. Acknowledge that those emotions are there, and move toward a solution to remedy them. Here's a hint: The solution to fixing those emotions is to talk through the difficult situation and find a solution.

If you avoid a difficult conversation, you will ultimately stunt the growth of your entire relationship. If you can't get past things that try to bring your relationship and emotions down, how are you going to grow moving forward? You have to get the problems out of the way in a conducive manner in order to truly move on with your relationship. Basically, avoiding difficult subjects is like putting a roadblock right under the tires of your relationship. It can't move forward if you don't get that roadblock out of the way, and moving backward is not something you want to do.

The bottom line is that if you don't face your difficult topics, they will remain difficult forever and just get worse with time. Don't avoid important things just because they are hard. Life is hard, but you have made it this far, and you should be proud of that. Take that pride and channel it into your conversations. Nothing is too big for you and your partner to handle. Your relationship is stronger than any challenge you will face, and if you believe that, you will both go far!

Look, I know it's scary. These conversations are scary, but you are stronger than this! Your relationship deserves that strength and courage, and your partner deserves it, too. Be the rock that your relationship can stand on, and initiate the conversations that must be had to move forward in your relationship. Tackling difficult conversations has a very good impact on your relationship, so fight them head-on! Don't short-circuit your relationship and unravel all of the progress you've made so far. Push past the grudges of difficult topics, and you will come out swinging. Your partner, and your relationship, will thank you. I promise!

CHAPTER 8
The Languages Of Love

The key to proper relationship communication is knowing how your partner expresses and receives love. This is a very strong communication of feelings, and it is a great indicator of how your partner can feel special. How we feel and express love is very closely linked to how we communicate and show affection in a relationship. These languages of love express the venues through which each individual feels, gives, and expresses love in their own way. Some people are entirely affiliated with one of these, and some are linked to many. Each person is unique, and the way they feel and express love is unique, too. You can love intimacy while feeling appreciated through acts of service, or you could simply feel love through the giving and receiving of gifts alone. Let's go over each of these love languages to see how love is communicated in each way, and which one may be calling out to you!

Physical Touch and Intimacy

Physical touch is what it sounds like. The love language of physical touch involves expressing or receiving your love in the form of skin-to-skin contact or general physical proximity where you can touch one another. It is a very passionate love language, and it is very common in those who have a very deep physical bond with their partner. It's also common in newlyweds, but it can be found in any walk of the relationship journey. Examples of physical touch include:
- Hugging
- Kissing
- Holding hands
- Sexual intimacy
- Massage
- Cuddling
- Pats on the head
- Placing a comforting hand on your partner's shoulder
- Leaning against your partner while sitting next to one another
- Playing footsies
- Sitting on your partner's lap.
- Gentle biting
- Rubbing or scratching your partner's back

Now, let's talk about how we can use physical touch to communicate love into your relationship! Remember how we talked about physical communication? This is the love child of physical communication! You can easily express your love and affection every day by using physical communication. When your partner is down in the dumps, placing a gentle hand on their shoulder can be enough to show that you care! When you are sad, your partner can express their understanding and love for you by giving you a tight, warm hug that translates so well into feelings of security, support, affection, and connectivity.

If you're feeling frisky, what better way to communicate it than physical touch? When you get hot and bothered, save the words for later and pepper your sweet partner with kisses and stimulating caresses. If you are feeling happy, hugs, and swinging your intertwined hands while you walk, communicate that very clearly. If you are stressed, there is no better way for your partner to love you than to give you a calm, relaxing massage to show that they care. See how easy it is to express your love and emotions with physical touch? It plays very well in our discussion on relationship communication, and it is a great way to feel close to your partner.

Quality Time Together

Quality time has a lot to do with simply knowing that your partner is there, in close proximity, and you revel in the presence of one another, whether or not you touch, talk, or interact, though those are a plus. People who respond to quality time like to plan movie nights, special dates, and game nights in order to woo their partners, and they normally feel the most connection when their partner does the same.

Examples of quality time include:
- Going on a dinner date
- Watching a movie together
- Planting a garden together
- Going on a walk together
- Visiting new and exciting places together
- Tackling obstacles as a team
- Playing games together
- Exercising with one another
- Playing a competitive video game together.
- Learning how to do something new together
- Finding new hobbies together, such as taking up an instrument, making pottery, rock climbing, archery, or cooking
- Build something together, such as a birdhouse or a bench
- Going on a drive together
- Doing everyday tasks together, such as cooking together or folding clothes together.
- Being in the same room, even if not talking, such as sitting next to each other and reading.

Now, how can we use the quality time to incorporate affection into our relationship communication? I'll show you how! Nonverbal communication is just as important in relationship communication as any other form. Quality time is where that comes into play. Choosing to be in the same room as your partner is its own unique form of communication. It communicates closeness, the security of being near one you love, and the message that you are not ignoring them. It makes your partner feel special, and it makes you happy just knowing that they are nearby.

If you or your partner are attuned to this love language, it is important to be able to pick up on their stance in the relationship. For instance, if you know that your partner shows affection by being near you, and they withhold that affection by staying distance, there may be something wrong. Reach out to them and ask why they don't feel as secure or loved in your presence to figure out why their expression of affection may have shifted. It may seem subtle at first, but if you truly understand your partner, you will be able to pick up on this.

Alternatively, if your partner spends more time around you than before, then you know your relationship is doing ok and that things are happy and full of love! If you and your partner enjoy quality time as your form of love, express it openly by spending as much time together as you can!

Sincere Words of Affirmation

Words of affirmation are popular for those who like to have stability and reliance on their partner in order to feel loved and appreciated. Being told thank you, I love you, and you look beautiful, etc. are incredibly uplifting for individuals who have an affinity to this love language. They are also often the first to give praise and to glow and smile upon receiving it.

Examples of words of affirmation include:
- Detailed compliments
- Saying thank you
- Telling your partner that you appreciate them and what they do
- Saying I love you
- Laughing at your partner's jokes
- Expressing that you are proud of your partner
- Cheering your partner on
- Letting your partner know you are there
- Telling your partner that they are safe in scary situations
- Leaving your partner cute love notes throughout the house
- Sending your partner sweet text messages, voice mails, emojis, and emails
- Saying you admire your partner or a certain quality of your partner

The love language of words of affirmation is probably the easiest love language you can utilize in your relationship communication. We communicate with words, after all! Use your love language to shower your partner with words of appreciation, and they will do the same back to you! Communicate everything in your heart openly and honestly, and you won't go wrong.

If you are down, your partner can cheer you up by expressing their love for you in words and saying how proud they are of you. If you are happy, your partner can rejoice right along with you and uplift your spirits even more! If you are scared, your partner can sit next to you and whisper in your ear that they are there, they will protect you, and that there is nothing to fear. The reassurance of words is the strongest way to make someone feel loved if they are attuned to words of affirmation. Use that to strengthen your relationship and sew affection into the dialogue you have with your partner.

Affectionate Gift Giving

Gift-giving can show up in many forms, but it involves the giving and receiving of items, handmade presents, and other forms of loving gifts. They are often quite crafty, either with creating items or cooking and show off their affections by communicating love by giving the things they make or buy to their loved ones. They also adore being surprised with little gifts, regardless of the value, and appreciate the thought of being remembered on special occasions.

Examples of gift-giving include:
- Making something by hand for your partner
- Buying your partner something they need, such as a new jacket, pair of shoes, or phone case
- Remembering your partner on their birthday with a thoughtful present
- Showering your partner with gifts during Christmas or similar holidays
- Creating a photo album of all of the memories you and your partner share
- Painting a mural or picture for your partner
- Buying your partner something useful or related to one of their hobbies, such as a new blender for someone who likes to cook or a vacuum for someone who likes to clean
- Buying new, comfortable pillows for the bed when you notice that your partner is having trouble sleeping at night
- Surprising your partner with a heartfelt gift, or something you know your partner wants
- Surprising your partner with their favorite meal or treat

Gift giving is a sweet way to communicate love in our relationships, and it is easy because there are so many ways that we can do it! You can give your partner a special gift on their birthday to communicate that you remembered. You can give your partner a sweet bouquet of flowers to tell them that you love them. You can bring them their favorite foods when they are sad to cheer them up and communicate that you care. You can bring them a giant teddy bear to snuggle when they are scared or sick. Communicate the effort you want to put into the relationship by making your partner a handmade present! You can even show a sign that you would like to get intimate by gifting your partner a new toy for the bedroom if you are into that kind of thing. All of these ways communicate your love in different ways, and there are many more! Get creative and find new ways to show your affection through gift-giving. It can be really fun!

Communicate your love by giving gifts on special occasions instead of simply speaking to acknowledge their importance. This makes the occasion feel more validated, and the gift feels more from the heart. Take some time to get to know your partner and figure out the kinds of things that they like, and you will open the door to many new possibilities in your relationship!

Devoted Acts of Service/Kindness

Acts of service are closely linked to the heart because when you do something for someone you love, it shows that you truly care for them and want to help out as much as you can. Doing something for someone you love can bring you so much joy if it is the way that you express and receive love, and it can be expressed in many different ways. People with this love language will often ask what they can do for their partner throughout the day to make it easier or more enjoyable for them. They show their love in every way through taking some time to take a load off for the other person. This can be small, simple tasks or large, extravagant ones. Each sign of affection holds its own message, and it can vary based on the level of affection you have for an individual, specific days or situations, and more!

Examples of acts of service/kindness include:
- Cooking your partner's favorite meal
- Bandaging a wound for your partner
- Driving your partner to an important meeting
- Bringing home your partner's favorite meal
- Surprising your partner by washing their car
- Repairing a broken item of your partner's
- Giving your partner a soothing massage
- Cleaning for your partner after a long day
- Making the bed
- Running to the store for your partner.
- Helping your partner finish a difficult task

Incorporate acts of service into your relationship dialogue easily by expressing care for your partner. If your partner is feeling stressed or overwhelmed from the day's work, show that you care by cleaning up some dishes or finishing a task for your partner that they were too busy to do. Show your partner your deepest love by helping them out when they are burdened. Take a weight off their shoulders and give them the support they need to show your deepest devotion and love.

Communicate compassion by cooking your partner a bowl of homemade soup when they are sick. If your partner is worried or frustrated about something, fix it. If they are sad, do something to make them happy. If they are tired, make them a nice cup of coffee or give them some time to take a nap. If they are feeling frisky, and you are too, show an act of service by initiating a steamy sexual encounter, complete with foreplay and lots of bodily kisses. There are so many ways to communicate acts of kindness into your relationship, specific to situations you feel need to be acted upon. You just have to find the right act to meet the situation, and the possibilities can be endless!

The Languages of Love Quiz

Now that we know what the languages of love are let's take a fun little quiz to see which one (or ones) you are most attuned to! That way, you will know how to communicate with your partner how you can feel the most loved and appreciated. Then, your partner can take it too so you can know how to shower them with love in a way that makes them happiest! Once you know your love language, you open up a whole world of possibilities for you and your relationship communication going forward. I hope you've enjoyed all of the advice I've given you so far!

For each statement, give a numerical value between one and five to indicate how much it speaks to you. In the end, tally up your totals based on the letter associated with each question to find out which love language is strongest for you! For instance, tally up your totals for each statement labeled P, Q, and so forth, and compare your totals for each letter.

1. P: I love to be kissed by my partner in order to feel cared for. _
2. Q: I enjoy watching a late-night movie with my partner, regardless of our distance to one another. _
3. G: I like receiving handmade gifts from my partner because it makes me feel appreciated. _
4. S: I like it when my partner helps me tackle a difficult task because it shows that they care. _
5. W: I love hearing sweet nothings whispered into my ear. _
6. P: I like to hold hands with my partner in public to feel that they want to be near to me physically at times. _
7. Q: I like to go on adventurous trips with my partner. _

8. G: I love receiving thoughtful surprises from my partner, such as a piece of clothing or jewelry that I have been eyeing. _
9. S: I like it when my partner opens the door for me. It makes me feel special. _
10. W: I love hearing phrases such as "I am proud of you," and "I appreciate you." _
11. P: I like receiving massages from my partner and feeling their hands on me. _
12. Q: I like to sit and eat dinner together with my partner. _
13. G: I love to receive thoughtful knick knacks from my partner to remind me of our relationship and how much it has meant to us. _
14. S: I enjoy coming home to a house cleaned by my partner after a long day. _
15. W: I like it when my partner sends me cute messages and emojis throughout the day to feel appreciated. _
16. P: I like to snuggle with my partner when we are in a room together. _
17. Q: I enjoy simply sitting in the same room as my partner, regardless of what we are doing. _
18. G: I enjoy it when my partner remembers me on special occasions by giving me gifts. _
19. S: It makes me feel good when my partner does little tasks for me throughout the day. _
20. W: I like hearing the words "I love you" more than the physical signs of love. _
21. P: I enjoy it when my partner touches me spontaneously throughout the day, such as with a quick hug, a kiss on the head, or a gentle caress. _
22. Q: I like to run daily errands with my partner just to be near to them. _
23. G: I like being surprised with sweets and/or my favorite foods by my partner. _
24. S: I enjoy it when my partner draws me a warm bath or makes the bed for me. _
25. W: I love being listened to after a particularly emotional day, and being told that everything is ok. _
26. P: I like to be comforted by a hug rather than words. _
27. Q: I feel comforted and safe most by the calming presence of my partner. _
28. G: When my partner gives me something, it makes me feel appreciated, and it gives our relationship security. _
29. S: When my partner does something to fix an issue for me, it makes me feel better. _

30. W: When someone tells me that everything is going to be ok, it means more than if someone were to give me a hug or try to fix it themselves. _
31. P: I get turned on by physical touch. _
32. Q: The presence of my partner gets me hot and bothered. _
33. G: Receiving a sexy gift from my partner gets me in the mood. _
34. S: When my partner gives me a back rub or makes me feel pampered, it makes me feel very romantic. _
35. W: I get stimulated very easily when my partner whispers steamy words into my ear. _
36. P: When I am feeling sad, I just want to be held. _
37. Q: When I am upset, I just want to be around my partner. _
38. G: When I am sad, gifts cheer me up more than anything. _
39. S: When I am not feeling happy, it makes me feel better when my partner does something thoughtful for me. _
40. W: When I am upset, my partner can cheer me up easily with kind words. _
41. P: I get excited about the future with my partner when we hold hands. _
42. Q: I can envision a life with my partner when we spend time together. _
43. G: I feel like my partner will be able to provide for me if I receive gifts. _
44. S: I can see myself marrying a partner who accomplishes tasks for me and helps me around the house. _
45. W: I love discussing the future with my partner. _
46. P: When I am feeling lonely, I want my partner to touch me to let me know that they are there. _
47. Q: When I am feeling lonely, all it takes is for my partner to step into the room to feel better. _
48. G: When I am lonely, it makes me feel better to receive a special gift from my partner. _
49. S: When I am feeling lonely, I like it when my partner drives me around. _
50. W: When I am feeling lonely, all I need to hear is that my partner is there for me. _

Here is how you scored:
If you tallied most for P, you are most likely attuned to *physical touch*.
If you tallied most for Q, you are most likely attuned to *quality time*.
If you tallied most for G, you are most likely attuned to *gift-giving*.
If you tallied most for S, you are most likely attuned to *acts of service*.
If you tallied most for W, you are most likely attuned to *words of affirmation*.

CONCLUSION

Thank you for reading *Relationship Communication*. I truly hope that it has given you ample insight into your relationship and the communication involved to keep it healthy and long-lasting! I also hope that it has been in at least a small way enlightening for your journey ahead as you traverse the waters of your relationship. As we know, those waters can be rocky, but through the guides in this book, I'm sure you can cross those waves with ease and come out floating on the waters of a healthy relationship! As I stated at the beginning of this book, my mission is to help you and your partner form deep bonds full of trust and open, honest communication. I hope I have achieved the goal of showing you how to reach those deep bonds and how to tackle any relationship endeavor that is tossed your way, through proper communication! If you have a stable, honest, and true relationship, you are on the right track! Just stay open, caring, empathetic, and smart about it, and you won't go wrong! Keep this book handy, if you want, in case you lose track along the way!

Alright, let's have a recap. In this book, we covered, over the course of the many detailed chapters and subchapters, the topics pertaining to relationship communication. These included the definition of relationship communication, what that means to you, and how you can use that communication in your personal relationships through various means. These means include physical touch, verbal communication, signing, body language, written words, and more! We then moved on to tackling the monster that is conflict resolution. We also found out many ways that we can fight that conflict head-on without attacking our partner!

After we accomplished that, we went on to discussing common relationship mishaps, including staying silent, suppressing emotions, being too much of a crutch, and jumping to conclusions. Whew, that was a lot! But we did it! We also found out how to tackle those mishaps so they don't stand in the way of the best relationship we can achieve in a healthy manner.

Then we got into the soft and mushy, but endearing, subject of empathy. We talked about how tuning into your partner's emotions, while not necessarily feeding off of them, can lead to a closer bond and a greater safety net of trust between the two of you. Then, we got steamy! We talked about communication's passionate and closely intertwined connection to intimacy in the bedroom. Finally, we talked about how to tackle difficult topics, and we also learned what the five languages of love are and how to express them!

The next step that I would recommend going forward is to follow the practices laid out in this book and to avoid the red flags I brought up as well. I hope that you can carry this through your relationship as an aid so that your relationships may blossom!

If you found this book helpful and worth your time, please leave a kind and honest review on Amazon. I always appreciate the sincere feedback so that I may improve upon my books over time. I also love to see what people think about my book and how it has helped them! Thank you again for choosing my book out of the many that circulate on the market today. I hope that it was worth your time!

DESCRIPTION

Would you like to grow closer to your partner? Are your relationships suffering from a lack of communication, pent up frustration, a plethora of misunderstandings, apparent disinterest, or other negative factors? What you need are proper communication skills! Relationship communication is incredibly important for strengthening your relational bonds, mending bridges, growing closer intimately, expressing emotions, preventing arguments, and so many other areas of a relationship. I'm here to help you unravel the complicated web of dialogue in a relationship, and I want to show you how you can apply communication skills in every possible aspect of your relationship so that it can bloom, strengthen, and grow in a healthy way. This book can lead you down a wonderful path in your relationship, and it can help you jump through the many hoops and hurdles that partnership brings to the table.

Topics I will bring to light in this book, and key points I will be addressing include:

- How to resolve conflicts
- How to prevent conflicts from occurring
- How to mend the damage caused by arguments and misunderstandings
- How to strengthen intimacy with verbal and bodily communication
- How to communicate your intimate needs and wants with touch, sound, and sight
- What it means to address consent, expectations, and hang-ups
- How to identify and utilize the five languages of love
- What relationship communication really means
- What relationship communication specifically means to you.
- The many outlets for communication, including physical, verbal, and more!
- Tackling common relationship mishaps
- Learning how to tackle and discuss difficult topics
- How to embrace and understand empathy
- And finally, how to talk to your partner!

Let this book be a guiding light that shines into your relationship and illuminates all of the wonderous opportunities available to you both. Let that revelation lead you down a path to growth, happiness, and love! With this book by your side, you can tackle anything that comes your way in your relationship, and you can resolve it with thoughtful, mature conversations. You will find that these conversations, and the methods you will learn in this book, are not as complicated as they may seem! You just have to learn how to navigate them, and this book will show you the way! Leaf through these chapters and open your eyes to a world of possibilities in your relationship!

Learn to let your walls down so you can open up to your partner, find out how trust and respect can become the glue that holds you two together, and express yourself in ways you never knew you could. You can do all of this, and more if you let yourself figure out how. I will show you how to understand and express all that is needed in a healthy and strong relationship if you will let me. All you have to do is allow yourself to be willing and receptive to the truth behind relationships and the honest communication involved. I know you can do it, and your partner will thank you for it!

www.ingramcontent.com/pod-product-compliance
Lightning Source LLC
Chambersburg PA
CBHW071454070526
44578CB00001B/336